HEALING † Touch MINISTRIES

FREEDOM NOW

For Drug & Alcohol Addictions

By Theo Johnson with Evelyn Diment

Scripture quotations, except where noted, are taken from the HOLY BIBLE, ENGLISH STANDANDARD VERSION, copyright © 2001 by Crossway Bibles, text edition copyright 2011.

Copyright © 1991 by Theo Johnson and Evelyn Diment

First printing December 1991
Second printing December 2015

Published by:

Lively Hope Ministries
P.O. Box 821961
Vancouver, WA 98682

ORDER BOOKS: livelyhopeministries@gmail.com

Visit us on the web:www.livelyhope.org

ISBN-13:978-1532989247

ISBN-10:1532989245

TABLE OF CONTENTS

A MESSAGE FROM EVELYN:

This book, which started out to be a handbook on how to minister to people with addictions and people who need the healing touch of the Lord Jesus Christ, seems to be getting bigger and bigger. I feel it is only fair for me to explain how I came by this information, apart from reading books, listening to tapes and hearing God for myself.

My father, whom I dearly loved, had a drinking problem, which caused much heartache and turmoil in our family. When I was fourteen, shortly after my father died, I stopped trying to cope with life and blamed it on God. From then on, as I tried to find happiness in a man and failed over and over, I kept blaming God for all my wrong choices. By the time I was 50, I was a hopeless alcoholic trying to find relief in the bottle. It really surprised me to find out that I myself had become a far worse drinker than my dad and a bigger nag than my mom, especially since I had made a solemn vow in my childhood that I'd never be like either one of them! Another thing that didn't help was my low self-esteem that began over an incident in the first grade, about a dress my mom made for me. Little did I know that the girl who made fun of my dress would become one of the women my handsome husband would have an affair with. She was superseded by my "best friend" who beat her to the punch--so you can see my life was off to a good start! At the age of 20, with my firstborn, Judy, I was on my own--betrayed, rejected, and needless to say, angry, hurt and very bitter.

One day, sitting in front of a TV with my cocktail, I happened upon the "Good News" program with Demos Shakarian, who was interviewing people God had set free from all kinds of addictions. At first I scoffed, but after two and a half hours of listening to their stories, I suddenly realized my glass was empty, and as usual when I waited too long between drinks, my body was alive with pain, nausea, the shakes, and my head was beginning to pound. I ran to the kitchen with only one thought on my mind--mix a BIG ONE--to get my body under control again. I was astounded to hear myself say, "God, if you're real and really did deliver those people, if You would do it for me, I'll serve You!" I had no idea what serving God meant, but as I made this incredible statement, it was as if something came over me and my arm went up in the air--vodka bottle and all--and down the sink went my "life support"! Right behind it came a sense of well-being, and I suddenly realized my stomach was no longer sick, my shakes had stopped, my head was no longer throbbing and the **pain was gone!** What a glorious, wonderful Heavenly Father we have!

In moments I was made whole--my physical body as well. From then on it was as if I had never drank--no withdrawals or D.T.s. You can see why my life now is spent sharing this glorious news and watching my Jesus heal, deliver and restore lives everywhere!

The prayers in this book are for everyone--not just the addicted, but any believer, new or long-standing, who is still bothered by old habits and feelings that cannot be shaken and which prevent the fullness of joy the new birth stands for. When you have finished these pages, I can promise you--"Old things will pass away and all things will be new."

Be brave--have an exciting adventure with Jesus!

A MESSAGE FROM THEO:

It has been my pleasure to work closely with Evelyn Diment over the years. I can attest to her love for people, especially those caught in addictions of every kind. Many people have heard her testimony and have been set free from addictions. Some of them have been immediately and permanently set free from alcoholism and drug addictions and are still dry and clean. For them we say hallelujah!! My concern, and Evelyn's heart, is for those who *did not have Evelyn's* experience. We used to think that God chose at random who He would set free and who He would not and we would never understand until we got to Heaven. How wrong we were.

After a number of years of studying addictions and the Scripture, we are convinced more than ever that God's will is for all of His people to be free from addictions of every kind! I don't know why some are set free immediately and others go through a process, but *I do know God has given a plan for **all to be free**.* He didn't come only to provide free passage to Heaven through His grace. He also came so that the captives could be set free! If you have been a captive to anything, he wants to set you free. He only needs your faith. What is faith? It's simply moving towards Jesus because you have hope that He can deliver you. Your willpower will never be enough. His power will be more than enough.

"Deliverance" is a word that needs an explanation. In the Church it has been abused by some and spoofed by others. On one hand there are those who claim that everything is caused by a demon, and on the other hand are those who doubt demons even exist. The former view releases people from personal responsibility and the later puts all the responsibility on the person. I believe neither is accurate and I am confident that Jesus has given us a pathway to healing for you that is balanced. He warned His disciples about the leaven of the Pharisees and the Sadducees. They were the extremists of His day. The Pharisees demanded supernatural signs and the Sadducees didn't believe in supernatural. Deliverance has suffered these extremes.

I believe setting you free from your addiction has three distinct phases. The Bible describes it as putting off your old man; being made new in the attitude of your mind; and putting on the new man. We have observed that these phases are sequential. In other words, it is necessary to put off the "old man" before it is possible to completely change how you think, and that you can't create a new self in Jesus until you change the way you think. *To be completely free will demand that you rely on God's help to change how you live, think and relate to Him.* You will find that being free entails a whole new life for you! God wants to change your spirit, mind and metabolism. To be a whole person, Jesus wants you to help Him minister to your spirit, mind and body. He came to save all of you.

It is for these reasons that Evelyn and I have come together to write this healing manual for you. We have observed people over the years, and have analyzed their successes and relapses. Some have gone through the process in this manual and have never looked back. Others have recycled through the process several times and finally were free. But through it all, the truths in this manual have become more and more clear to us. Therefore, be careful when you feel the first phase of freedom. It often is euphoric! The craving disappears and people feel they are finished with this group. *That usually is not the case.* Remember, you have had an addictive mindset all these years. Your euphoria will be short lived if you don't stay around long enough to allow us to help you change it.

We love you and pray for you daily. Hang on to the hand of Jesus tightly through the next few months. He will never leave you.

THE ADDICTED PERSON

If you are the typical person, it probably was very difficult for you to come to this point in your life where you finally admitted your addiction. We all have been there. We all have said we could quit any time we wanted to, and we all have made vows to ourselves until we grew tired of making them. Maybe you were one of those who thought it really wasn't all that bad until your family left you or you lost your job. Where ever you started, and for whatever reason you took that first drink or first hit, it is for certain *no one in this group set out to be an addict*! We all thought we could stop when we chose to.

When we finally admitted that whatever we were turning to was bad for us, and that we were out of control, we saw we were addicted. But, by then it was too late. How in the world did we get here?

Most researchers today agree that drugs are not the problem. THE PROBLEM LIES WITHIN US.[1]

While it is true that in alcoholism there is a definite genetic predilection to alcohol in some people that will cause a drinker to become an instant alcoholic, most people who become addicted to chemicals are already addicted to something else. I can understand that may sound like a pretty radical statement to you, because we have always looked at "addicts" as those living on the streets, or under bridges down town. Even the alcoholic didn't look at himself as an addict until recently. But America is an addicted society. One current writer has even gone so far to observe that *all* addictions are simply a response to a dysfunctional society. He states that families and society in America are so painful that Americans turn to chemicals to numb out their pain.[2] It was to be only temporary at first until they could figure out how to cope with their problems, but along the way they never found the skills or the time to cope and so became hooked. Many of us turned to food, sex, work, adrenalin, and religion--all the "safe" addictions--before we finally turned to chemicals.

What you must understand about your healing is that it will take a complete change in how you think, relate to yourself, live, and fulfill emotional, physical and spiritual needs, *because chances are, you have an addictive personality. Alcohol or drugs were added because your other coping skills were not working.* An addict has a belief system and a personality that is addictive. He doesn't realize it because it has been with him so long. He may think it is normal.

What is an addictive personality? We will go into this in more detail, but for now it is people who will not or cannot accept their limitations and insist that life ought to be "a ten". This drives them to look for quick fixes and insist that they are omnipotent (all powerful) which keeps them from facing their inner turmoil. They use activities or chemicals to soothe this inner turmoil.

REMEMBER: ADDICTION = ANYTHING YOU KEEP DOING EVEN WHEN IT IS BAD FOR YOU.

Think back through your life. List the things you were doing even though they were bad for you before you started drinking or using drugs:

1

Before we continue in this healing manual, it is important to understand your enemy. To fight him, you must understand his tactics. Otherwise, you will be like a man in a dark room swatting mosquitoes--you will only be able to react but it will be too late.

REMEMBER: ADDICTION DOESN'T MEAN YOU DO IT EVERY DAY. IT DOES MEAN IT IS DESTRUCTIVE IN YOUR LIFE BUT YOU DO IT ANYWAY.

HOW DO I KNOW I'VE BECOME ADDICTED?

There are well-known signs of addiction. They are called the "Four Cardinal Signs of Addiction".[3] Look at these symptoms closely and make any comments about your life in the space provided.

1. **Obsession:** There is a "command from within" that many people who are addicted feel. It is as if their body or something "other" than themselves have to have the chemical. They think about it much of the time. There often is a preparation ritual they go through to get out of their depression or the negative moods before they actually use the chemical.

2. **Negative consequences:** There always, eventually, are bad consequences for using this method to escape our pain. It usually has to do with our health, but it can also have to do with our relationships or work, but we do it anyway.

3. **Lack of control:** After we continue in this behavior for a while, we come to a place where we are out of control. At first, we don't think we are out of control and can stop any time we want. There often are promises to stop at some future date, but when we get there we can't seem to stop. At this point, the more we try to use our will power the worse our addiction becomes.

4. **Denial:** Some people have termed denial a "micro-psychosis," because there is a break with reality. They have built up such a sophisticated belief system to keep their drug of choice that they are blind to the negative consequences of the drug in their lives. They often are very defensive when loved ones try to tell them.

THE ADDICTIVE LIFESTYLE

HOW DID YOU GET HERE? As we said earlier, nobody in this group set out to be controlled by someone or something destructive in their life. It is a mystery to many of us how we could have let this happen. You have read Evelyn's life story and may identify with it in certain areas. But if you look closely, you will see a predictable path to her alcoholism. Since the path is predictable, it is reversible. Therefore, for you to be permanently free from your addiction, it is important for you to understand how you got here, so that you can resist old patterns if they try to raise their head again. If you don't understand, you are setting yourself up. Hosea 4:6 "My people are destroyed from lack of knowledge."

Let's look at the path to addiction from several angles so that you might understand *why* we are going to ask you to do certain things in this manual. Remember, we said that addictions are most often an effort to soothe the turmoil within us. Some have called this DIS-EASE because there is a lack of "ease" within us. How did that get there? It most often started in childhood when we were "imprinted" by significant events or people who did not meet our needs or caused trauma in our young lives. As young people, we formed certain "rules" to live by in a reaction to that pain and ingrained them in our lives by acting them out. This became our addictive lifestyle. It looks like this:

Step 1.----------------> Step 2.------------------> Step 3.------------> Step 4.--------------------->Step 5.

First Imprint	Formation of Addictive Mindset	Ingraining	Second Imprint	Addiction
TRAUMA & UNMET NEEDS cause inner turmoil. The person adapts rules to live by that he believes will solve his turmoil. Some of these are listed in the next column.	✓ I should be perfect. ✓ I should be all powerful. ✓ I should always be able to get what I want. ✓ I should not have pain in my life. ✓ I am powerless. ✓ Feelings are dangerous ✓ External things will give me all the power I need. ✓ Image is everything ✓ I should meet my needs indirectly. ✓ I'm worthless ✓ I'm not lovable.	ACTING OUT BELIEFS Acting on a belief will become part of you whether it is true or not. Turmoil grows--the rules are not working.	These are activities or chemicals I have learned that give temporary relief to my inner turmoil: Alcohol Drugs Food Work Sex Adrenalin (crisis) Exercise Television Religion Relationships Approval Cutting Cigarettes Gambling Pornography Spending Computer games	There are activities or chemicals I use even when I know it is bad for me--I can't stop: Alcohol Drugs Food Work Sex Adrenaline (crisis) Exercise Television Religion Relationships Approval Cutting Cigarettes Gambling Pornography Spending Computer games

Now, look at the listed sequence of events very carefully. Do you see that the ultimate destruction of addiction is ONLY A WAY TO ESCAPE FACING THE REAL ROOT OF OUR PROBLEM--THE PAIN OF UNMET NEEDS AND TRAUMA IN OUR LIVES? *This truth is very important for you to face because if you don't, you will continue to seek the mythical "quick fix" and only do more harm to yourself and your loved ones.* We have to admit that we have tried to anesthetize our inner turmoil and have unwittingly become addicted to the anesthesia. Numbing out a toothache doesn't cure the toothache, it only postpones the pain. Something has to be *done* about the *cause* of the toothache.

How did you get out of control? When people have lived a number of years without ever facing the lack of peace they have inside, they will predictably come to a time in their life when they decide they will do something about it. If they have the good fortune to be tied into a healing church or good counseling, they will find that peace. But if not, they will turn to whatever has given temporary relief in the past. They will go through the following steps.[4] Look at these steps closely and make comments about your loss of control along the way:

1. **Infatuation:** During times of stress, grief, loneliness, or any other negative emotion we haven't learned to deal with, there begins a growing infatuation with the memory of pleasurable experiences with chemicals or activities. It may have happened at a party or alone or with friends, but you remember the pleasure.

If you are one of those people who have not faced the reason for the lack of ease within you, your brain has been looking for some way to ease the pain. In fact, many researchers believe that your brain may actually misinterpret this substance as having survival value, especially if it meets unmet needs. The body uses this substitute for feeling whole or complete.

2. **Honeymoon:** There is typically a time when you feel power. You have done something about those negative feelings. While using, you feel you finally have found the quick fix to your problems.

3. **Betrayal:** After a time of using the drug, you notice it no longer brings the needed results. You have built a tolerance for the drug and have to use more to achieve the same results.

The drug has now replaced any coping skills you once had, and in fact has become your coping mechanism as the quick fix.

There is a growing sense of shame and inadequacy because the drug is now in control.

Denial sets in. It is partly a defense mechanism to defend your low self-esteem and partly because you have lost the ability to realistically evaluate the original problem or the negative effects of the addiction.

4. **Crash:** You thought you could recapture the honeymoon, but because your body built up a tolerance, that was never a possibility. In fact, there can never again be the high you felt at first.

Even at the first stage, you were trapped because you thought you could quit at any time "you *really* wanted to." But by now, almost anything triggers your cravings. Willpower has no effect at all.

You are starting to fear withdrawal. Because of this fear it becomes easier to continue using.

Your body quit making the "feel good" neurotransmitters on its own because you had given it a substitute. Therefore, when you tried to quit the drug, there was a real "down" that would cause you to suffer withdrawals and you would use whatever your drug of choice was to get "up" again.

Drugs affect neurotransmitters in three known ways:[5]

A. They are structurally similar to our natural "feel good" neurotransmitters, like endorphins, so they are able to attach to the receptor sites of the nerve endings and give the same "high". Morphine and endorphins are the best known example. If morphine is present much of the time, your body automatically reduces production of endorphins, letting the drug become a substitute. The problem with this is that when you try to withdraw from the drug, since your body has quit making endorphins, their absence causes a profound "down" or "crash".

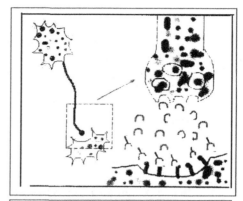

B. The drug interferes with reuptake of our natural neurotransmitters. Consequently, your body interprets that more is needed and manufactures more, which stays at the receptor site to stimulate. This affects the amount of raw material available to make the neurotransmitter, so when the drug is removed, the brain isn't able to make up the deficit, and again there is a crash.

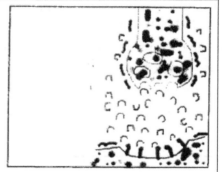

C. The drug is able to combine with other biochemical in your body and then mimic and/or interfere with the receptor site as in our first two examples.

5. **A Slave:** You are obsessed with the drug now. You have lost your ability to cope in any other way. You are out of control.

You probably fluctuated between your before-using ritual, and stark terror. You kept using because you feared change.

We have good news for you! Jeremiah 29:11 "For I know the plans I have for you, declares the LORD, plans for welfare and not for evil, to give you a future and a hope."

There is life after addiction. Your life is not forever ruined. You can have the feeling of well-being that can only come by being set free from your addiction. But you must settle something right here and right now! *Your will power will never be enough and never was the answer.* Give up any notion here and now that you can overcome this by yourself. You need God in your life in a new and fresh way that will keep you free for the rest of your life. He isn't a cosmic supermarket where you come to buy your freedom or your peace. He won't play magic with you. But He is a loving and *miraculous* Father who will set you free when you are *rightly* related to Him. Therefore, we *must* spend some time understanding His plan for us and satan's plan for us so that we can see how to be related to Him in the right way before we go on in this manual. Please, do not skip over this section lightly. It is foundational to your healing.

SATAN'S MASTER PLAN

How did addiction come into this world? How do men and women become slaves to the things we have been talking about? Well it is as old as the hills. In fact, we see the plan laid out from the foundations of the earth. Read the text closely from Genesis, and observe my comments on the left hand side of the page:

---

1. satan creates an imaginary unmet need and trauma in Eve's mind. He had to do this to get the addiction cycle going.

Gen 3:1-13 Now the serpent was more crafty than any other beast of the field that the LORD God has made. He said to the woman, "Did God actually say, 'You shall not eat of any tree in the garden'?"

---

2. satan lies to Adam and Eve by twisting what God actually said. He later tries the same tactic on Jesus in the wilderness.

3. satan sets the trap for every addiction:

A. QUICK FIX

B. YOU SHOULD BE LIKE GOD (all powerful)

And the woman said to the serpent, "We may eat of the fruit of the trees in the garden,

but God said, 'You shall not eat of the fruit of the tree that is in the midst of the garden, neither shall you touch it, lest you die.'"

But the serpent said to the woman, "You will not surely die.

For God knows that when you eat of it your eyes will be opened, and you will be like God, knowing good and evil."

---

4. Adam and Eve acted on the lie.

So when the woman saw that the tree was good for food, and that it was a delight to the eyes, and that the tree was to be desires to make one wise, she took of its fruit and ate, and she also gave some to her husband who was with her, and he ate.

---

5. Adam and Eve felt shame and guilt for the first time.

Then the eyes of both were opened, and they knew that they were naked. And they sewed fig leaves together and made themselves loincloths.

And they heard the sound of the LORD God walking in the garden in the cool of the day, and the man and his wife hid themselves from the presence of the LORD God among the trees of the garden.

---

6. DENIAL. Adam blames God and his wife and she blames the snake. They would not face themselves and refused to take responsibility.

But the LORD God called to the man and said to him, "Where are you?"

And he said, "I heard the sound of you in the garden, and I was afraid, because I was naked, and I hid myself."

He said, "Who told you that you were naked? Have you eaten of the tree of which I commanded you not to eat?"

The man said, "The woman whom you gave to be with me, she gave me fruit of the tree, and I ate."

Then the LORD God said to the woman, "What is this that you have done?" The woman said, "The serpent deceived me, and I ate."

HOW DOES ADAM AND EVE'S FALL RELATE TO YOU?

You might go back in the manual now and review the clinical stages of addiction and compare it with the fall of Adam and Eve (pages 3 & 4). You will notice striking similarities. That is because God's Word is true. Modern science is discovering what has been in the Bible for thousands of years.

What similarities do you see?

Your own addictive cycle: Let's look at the addictive cycle laid out in Genesis on paper. It would be good for you to start thinking with us now about how this fits in your life. You may have to really think but it is worth it. Remember, unless you understand your enemy, you can't beat him.

STEP 2: ADDICTIVE MIND SET

Quick Fix: There must be an easier way.
I'll find the answer some day.

I should be like God:
I should be in control of all.
I must be in control or I'm bad.

demonic energy

STEP 1: ADDICTIVE ROOT

Unmet needs: Growing up in a dysfunctional home.

Trauma: Abuse in history: emotional wounds; suppressed and/or repressed emotions.
These are things that cause your inner turmoil

anger and/or fear

STEP 5: DENIAL, BLAME THE ADDICTIVE ESCAPE

I need it because of the stress of my job.
If my husband wasn't such a problem, I wouldn't be so nervous and have to drink.
I'll try the same behavior again; maybe it will work this time (magical thinking)

STEP 3: INGRAINING; ADDICTIVE LIFE STYLE

The things you do to ease the lack of ease:
Use drugs or alcohol; A lack of self-worth; impulsive; friends are users; no coping skills; living in unreal world; running from pain.

STEP 4: THE CRASH

SHAME·RAGE·GRIEF·FEAR·NUMBNESS
This is the stage where addicted people fail. They need to accept GRACE from God for themselves. Instead, they try harder and make another vow. This makes the addiction worse because it adds to their inner turmoil.

As we have observed people coming out of their bondages over the years, we have seen this pattern over and over and over. It is nothing new. But what you have to see is THAT THE DRUG OF YOUR CHOICE *IS NOT THE PROBLEM*. You only have to look at studies done on early alcohol and drug treatment centers to see that truth. For years it was thought that if you took users out of their environments, detoxified them for thirty days, they would not go back to alcohol or drugs. Medications were given to make the withdrawals tolerable, some coping skills were taught, and usually some help was given to help them feel better about themselves. But the success rate was horrible! Finally, people started observing that drugs were not really the root problem. They concluded that Americans are trying to anesthetize their pain and that most of them do not know the source of their pain.[6]

The addictive personality described on the previous page is you. You have been running from your pain. You feel alone and that no one is able to help you or care about you. TAKE HEART! GOD HAS A PLAN FOR YOU!

Well, if the alcohol or drug I'm using is not really the problem, then what is? I'm glad you asked. Look at the addiction cycle again on page 7. THE ADDICTIVE ROOT is the problem. It has to be rooted out. It only grows bad fruit.

Another factor is your ADDICTIVE MIND SET. There are things that you believe about life right now that you will no longer believe after you are well. These beliefs have been with you so long they seen quite natural and comfortable. But they are your enemy. They also must be rooted out, because you are headed toward your most dominant thought right at this moment.

But, by far the biggest factor is YOUR RELATIONSHIP WITH GOD. You must once and for all quit trying to do things your own way. Like Adam and Eve, you have tried to be like God. It wasn't intentional as it was for Lucifer, but remember that the quick fix and that idea that you should be a 10 just like God, started this whole mess. *That perspective on life will separate you from the life of God and cause you to cooperate with Lucifer even when you don't want to.*

Then what is a proper perspective of yourself and God? It is simply this: **Accept right now that you are a 5 and God is a 10. You are powerless over this addiction and always will be. Accept that your world has been out of touch with reality. It has been a mirage you have been trying to capture, and has caused you a great deal of frustration and pain. As long as you think you are omnipotent, you will continue to try to control your addiction too. Reconcile yourself to the fact that it is *only when you learn to live with being a 5 that you become human and God can be a 10 in your life!* Then you will be living in a realistic world and God can help you. To do this is to accept GRACE. It is grace that will set you free--not willpower.**

You may be saying right at this moment, "Well you're wrong! I don't think I'm a 10. I have a terrible self-image!" You are right--you do have a terrible self-image. But the reason you do is that you are comparing yourself to a mythical 10! You have withdrawn into yourself.

Or you may be saying, "I don't think I'm a 10! I'm always trying to help people. I'm the most humble person you would want to meet." I know you look at life that way, but why are you constantly trying to get everyone to like you? Why do you try to change people to make you feel better when only God can change them? Do you see? There are many ways people try to be God in their own lives and in the lives of other people. The irritation and frustration of doing so drives them to chemicals.

GOD'S MASTER PLAN FOR YOUR LIFE

If will power is not going to set you free from your addiction, then what should you do? It is very simple, but will take your commitment. It will demand that you change how you relate to God, yourself and others. It will demand changing how you think and meet your needs. But don't be afraid. Jesus Christ, your Creator, is going to be with you the whole way.

God's plan for you is to unravel satan's master plan in your life. You have a very good idea of how that happened from reading the previous pages. It would be good to go back now and review the steps of addiction on pages 3 & 7 and compare it with the healing model below:

Stopping demonic energy

STEP 4: CORRECTING ADDICTIVE MIND SET

There is No Quick Fix: This manual will help you renew your perspective on life in a healthy way.
I should Not be like God: This manual will help you sort out all the ways you have tried to take responsibility for things you are humanly not able to carry.

STEP 3: HEALING THE ADDICTIVE ROOT

Meet your needs: Learn how to be good to yourself without harming yourself or others.

Healing the Trauma: You will finally be able to turn your turmoil over to The only one who is built to carry it--**God**. There usually is a great relief after this step.

STEP 1: COMING OUT OF DENIAL; Removing the Blame

Because of God's GRACE, you will be able to face your actions. YOU ARE NOT A BAD PERSON BECAUSE OF ADDICTION. You will take responsibility for NOW and YOURSELF

STEP 5: INGRAINING NEW LIFE STYLE

Because of the previous steps, you will be more able to change your lifestyle: You will learn how to cope with life in healthy ways that will forever change your life.

STEP 2: START WALKING IN GRACE:

You will learn the freedom and joy of being human. If you fall, God will help you get up if you ask Him. He will never tire of you. This reality will keep you from trying to be God again. It will keep you from building up more turmoil inside because you can give the rage, and shame and fear to God.

At this time, we suggest you go ahead and read the rest of this manual in one setting if you can. We want you to see the overall battle plan. We have learned that the more you can understand about your addiction, the better you will be able to overcome it. After you have read through the manual and have a good grasp of your path of healing, come back to page 11 and start with Step 1.

We have learned that unraveling satan's plan in your life and implementing God's plan is a step-by-step process. Also, the steps are sequential--that is, you cannot start in the middle of these steps and expect to come to complete freedom. At the same time, we realize that this cycle has a great deal of energy in your life and that to slow it down will take some immediate action. Namely, **abstinence from your drug** of choice. You cannot think straight or function physiologically unless you are detoxified from the influences of the drug. BECAUSE OF THIS TRUTH, WE FEEL IT IS WISE TO MOVE THROUGH STEPS 1 TO 3 AS QUICKLY AS POSSIBLE. *IF YOU HAVE TO BE DETOXIFIED, DO SO!* Don't feel bad about doing so. Your life is at stake.

A word of encouragement before you start: We have observed over the years that few go through this process we are going to cover in this manual without ever looking back. For most, however, your healing will not be a straight-line improvement upward and onward. It has helped us to see that most people will recycle several times through the healing steps we are going to describe as shown in the diagram to the right. As you come to healing, new layers may come off, and *it will seem as if you are regressing in your healing.* Take heart; that usually isn't the case. For instance, if you find yourself battling old thoughts, resist looking at is as a failure, but as an opportunity to reveal more of your addictive thought patterns that may have remained hidden. Understanding this will greatly improve your healing process. Much of our turmoil is deeply repressed and doesn't come out in the beginning. Keep at it. Many people will go through this manual 2 or 3 times and go through the "housecleaning" more than once. That isn't a sign of failure, but of recognizing reality.

Healing Progress

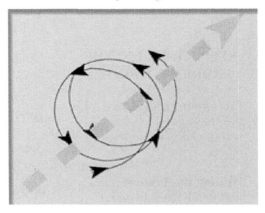

BE COMMITTED TO THE GROUP: You cannot beat this by yourself. Remember, that is a sign of "omnipotence". You need the group and the leaders of the group. If you are going to go through the healing process of Freedom Now, attend this group. It is not recommended that you go to several drug or alcohol groups at once, especially if they have conflicting philosophies.

STEP 1. COMING OUT OF DENIAL--REMOVING THE BLAME

DENIAL

Denial always comes before blame. It is a handy little defense mechanism we have invented to keep from having to face the real problem. Poor little Fred in our cartoon is hurting himself, but do you think he will admit it? No way! It doesn't matter if blood is running down his face, he has a tremendous headache, his nose is big and red as a melon, and that everyone else says he has a problem--he's OK! Just ask him.

Fred isn't looking at the facts because he doesn't want to pull the arrow out. He's afraid it will be too painful. He's miserable, but at least it's familiar. He doesn't understand it isn't going to hurt anywhere nearly as bad as he thinks. In fact, the freedom he is going to feel is going to be so different from how he's lived for years, that it will cause him to live in entirely new ways.

"What are you lookin' at!?"

BLAME

Blame is a way to shift the shame to someone or something else. Adam had the audacity to blame God *and* his wife and Eve blamed the snake. It will always keep you from finally and forever removing the thorn from your flesh. Its like having a rock in your shoe, but blaming your pain on ill-fitting shoes. Like Bossy, we often blame our rage, depression, blues, and shame on people or things *we can see* beacause we are not aware of the true souce of our pain. When we cant change our environment or the people around us, we have always turned to the one thing we know will anesthetize us. For a while it made us feel like we were in control. Bossy thinks she is controlling the situation, but there is *nothing Rufus can do about it because it's Bossy's problem.* BOSSY MUST START TELLING HERSELF THE TRUTH! That is the way it is with us.

"You know, Rufus, every time I talk to you I get this pain."

THIS STEP REQUIRES YOU TO DO SEVERAL IMMEDIATE AND DECISIVE THINGS:

1. OWN YOUR OWN EMOTIONS: It is rarely true that others **make** us mad or depressed or have any other emotion that causes us to drink. *We choose to feel that way.* Our addicive mind set causes us to blame others or our environment, but the truth is that it is an escape. You may not believe what we are saying at this moment, but believe us when we say it is true.

Further, when we blame others for our negative emotions, *we will try to control those people.* If we are a strong personality, we will try to dominate and if we are not as strong, we will try to manipulate. If we are ever going to break free from this vicious cycle, *we must start today BY TAKING RESPONSIBILITY FOR NOW AND FOR OURSELVES.*

2. TELL SOMEONE: There *must be accountability*. Pride was the original sin for Lucifer and will keep you in the "omnipotence" mode. You cannot fight this by yourself. It takes humbleness and accountability. This group is a given for accountability, but pick one other person. It is especially effective if that person is one you have been trying to control. To not tell yourself and someone else the truth, is to give the addiction cycle power in your life. You must do the opposite of what gives it energy.

Below is a log for you to record your emotions and how you act them out.

Negative Emotions	What I usually do to try to control, manipulate, or cause change in others so that I feel better.	Who is usually involved	Person I am going to tell Date:

What has this drug cost you? Have you ever really looked at the costs to you? It is always good to write things down on paper. There is something about taking action regarding your thoughts that seals your conviction to continue in your healing. Below is a log to record what this drug of choice has cost you in many areas of your life. The purpose is to help you evaluate and come further out of denial. Many will say, "Oh, it really wasn't that bad," until they look at it on paper.

What My Drug of Choice Has Cost Me Over The Years

Money	Lost Friends	Lost Time	Lost Family

Lost Chances	Lost Mental Abilities	Lost Health	Lost Emotional & Spiritual Health

Was it worth it?

STEP 2. WALKING IN GRACE

It is time for us to stop and make sure you are rightly related to God before we go on. You see, if Adam and Eve would have relied on the grace of God instead of the judgment of God, we probably wouldn't be in the fix we are today. They were afraid to admit what they had done. Of course, we will never be able to play that "video" until we get to Heaven and ask God what would have happened.

GRACE IS GETTING SOMETHING WE DON'T DEVERVE. **Whenever you find yourself relating to God in any other way than a grace mode, you will find yourself avoiding Him, or doing the things you really don't want to do.** Therefore, it is a matter of life or death that you understand His grace because you need Him in your life. You can't avoid Him and get well. You will find yourself doing the very things you don't want to do. That you've already proven. You need to understand God as He really is.

You will understand grace at a heart level someday. For now, I am simply going to list some scripture with notes. I am going to list them according to God's plan for us in chronological order.

Notice that the text says let us create man in our image. Keep that in mind. God is God the Father, God the Son and God the Holy Spirit. Man and woman are created in God's image. That means you are also made like God. You have a body; that is like God the Son, Jesus Christ, who came and walked among us and died for our sins. You have a spirit; you can't see it but it is real which is like the Holy Spirit. And you have an intelligence and presence about you that no one can see which is in authority; that is like God the Father. Just as we are not three distinct persons, neither is God nor is it true that we or He are so intertwined into one that we cannot be separated. Parts of this truth will always be a mystery, but it is very close to reality.

Gen 1:26-27 Then God said, "Let us make man in our image, after our likeness. And let them have domination over the fish of the sea and over the birds of the heavens and over the livestock and over all the earth and over every creeping thing that creeps the earth."

So God created man in his own image, in the image of God he created him; male and female he created them.

Christianity is not a religion. All religions have one thing in common—man has to work at getting close to God. He has to meditate to understand a "higher meaning" to life or take a pilgrimage or live a restricted life.

*Christianity rests on one audacious and earth shaking claim--**Jesus Christ is God, God the Son. He came to die for our sins so that we don't have to be perfect to be close to God anymore.** He isn't a nice man or a prophet or a philosophical free thinker. He isn't a whipping boy that God decided to pick out as a sacrifice for our sins. He is God. He has always been there from the foundations of the earth and gave His life willingly. That is GRACE. You or I, no matter how good we've tried to be, don't merit that.*

John 1:1-4 In the beginning was the Word, and the Word was with God, and the Word was God.

He was in the beginning with God

All things were made through him, and without him was not anything made that was made.

In him was life, and the life was the light of men.

To prove He was God, He fulfilled every prophesy written about Him hundreds of years before, on time to the day and hour. Further, He rose from the dead and walked earth for 40 days. Over 500 people saw Him. He then bodily ascended into Heaven. The mathematical chances of Jesus; meeting every prophesy on time, *even if He tried to manipulate events,* is astronomical. Add to that the probability that 12 men, His disciples, would all go to terrible deaths in separate parts of the world to protect a hoax, is astronomical in itself. No, we have God the Son who stepped down off His throne and walked among us for 33 ½ years and lived like us, felt with us and died for us. We serve a God who has cried, suffered and laughed with us.

John 1:14 And the Word became flesh and dwelt among us, and we have seen his glory, glory as of the only Son from the Father, full of grace and truth.

John 1:17 For the law was given through Moses; grace and truth came through Jesus Christ.

But why? If He didn't have to go to the cross, then why did He? **So that you and I can be free!** Look at verse 15 of Romans 5. Remember our addiction cycle from Genesis? Paul is saying that sin came into the world through Adam. That process started the world down the path to be slaves to everything but God. Man has been trying to fill his life with everything but God. But man hasn't known *how* to get close to God, so he is caught between a rock and a hard place.

But God had a plan from the beginning! He placed a Jesus-shaped void in our lives. He came to show us what God the Father is like! Look at verse 18 of John. Jesus has shown the true love of the Father for us. He came to break the cycle.

What difference does that make? A whole lot! **You cannot really love yourself unless you are convinced that someone greater loves you. Much of your insecurity and inner turmoil comes from your doubts about this fact.**

When the "child" within you starts accepting that it's OK to be a 5; that we are children, and the only 10 in the whole universe loves us *so* much that He would willingly suffer and die for us *just the way we are **right now**, it transforms our lives.* You don't have to white knuckle it anymore. You can accept where you are today and trust Him to help you through it.

John 1:18 No one has ever seen God; the only God, who is at the Father's side, he has made him known.

Rom 5:1 Therefore, since we have been justified by faith, we have peace with God through our Lord Jesus Christ.

Rom 5:6 For while we were still weak, at the right time Christ died for the ungodly.

Rom 5:15 But the free gift is not like the trespass. For if many died through one man's trespass, much more have the grace of God and the free gift by the grace of that one man Jesus Christ abounded for many.

The "law" was an impossible set of rules and regulations the Jews had to keep to be rightly related to God. Paul is saying it was given to show mankind that he cannot be a 10. He can never be rightly related to God by trying harder. The only way he can be rightly related to God is to accept His gift of grace. It cost Him quite a bit.

Romans 5:20-21 Now the law came in to increase the trespass, but where sin increased, grace abounded all the more,

so that, as sin reigned in death, grace also might reign though righteousness leading to eternal life through Jesus Christ our Lord.

When you understand how much grace cost God and, therefore, how much He must love you just as you are, it has to affect you. **If you take it lightly, it won't.**
If you identify Christ, then you will realize He put your Adam nature to death when He went to the cross for you. Your Adam nature is the part of you that doesn't want to obey God's prescription for life and wants to fulfill itself with drugs, alcohol or anything else besides God.

Romans 6:1-4 What shall we say then? Are we to continue in sin that grace may abound?

By no means! How can we who died to sin still live in it?

Do you not know that all of us who have been baptized into Christ Jesus were baptized into his death?

We were buried therefore with him by baptism into death, in order that, just as Christ was raised from the dead by the glory of the Father, we too might walk in newness of life.

To accept the power of God's grace in your life, you must count as dead that part of you that wants to be God. Something has to die before new life can begin. God is *not* saying you have to become a zero and that you are to be a lifeless robot. He is saying the "old part" of you, that Adam part of you that wants to do everything its own way, must die. In other words, *accept you're a 5 so He can be a 10 in your life.*

Romans 6:6 We know that our old self was crucified with him in order that the body of sin might be brought to nothing, so that we would no longer be enslaved to sin.

Romans 6:11 So you also must consider yourselves dead to sin and alive to God in Christ Jesus.

"Sin" is missing the mark. It will eventually kill or at least maim us. Paul is saying that out of gratitude and just good common sense, offer yourself to God instead of those things that destroy your life. YOU HAVE TO REPLACE A NEGATIVE WITH A POSITIVE.

Romans 6:13 Do not present your members to sin as instruments for unrighteousness, but present yourselves to God as those who have been brought from death to life, and your members to God as instruments for righteousness.

GRACE will set you free. If you try to continue to "be perfect," sin will master you.

Romans 6:14 For sin will have no dominion over you, since you are not under law but under grace.

Now Paul starts to explain *why* it is fruitless to continue to make vows to ourselves, to be harder on ourselves, and all the things people do trying to get off drugs, food or any other addiction.

The Law of Paradoxical Intention: It is a law of human nature that simply states that *a negative trait cannot be permanently and genuinely changed by a negative command.* Every human being and every addict has felt its sting. It is a paradox (doesn't seem logical) because the intent is to change, hence the term "paradoxical intention."

In fact, Paul is saying the more he tried to do what the law says not to do, he finds himself doing it. Have you ever been there?

Rom 7:5 For while we were living in the flesh, our sinful passions, **aroused** by the law, were at work in our members to bear fruit for death.

Rom 7:8-10 But sin, seizing an opportunity through the commandment, **produced** in me all kinds of covetousness. For apart from the law, sin lies dead.
I was once alive apart from the law, but when the commandment came, sin came alive and I died.
The very commandment that promised life proved to be death to me.

Rom 7:15-24 For I do not understand my own actions. For I do not do what I want, but I do the very thing I hate.
Now if I do what I do not want, I agree with the law, that it is good.
So now it is no longer I who do it, but sin that dwells within me.
For I know that nothing good dwells in me, that is, in my flesh. For I have the desire to do what is right, but not the ability to carry it out.
For I do not do the good I want, but the evil I do not want is what I keep on doing.
Now if I do what I do not want, it is no longer I who do it, but sin that dwells within me.
So I find it to be a law that when I want to do right, evil lies close at hand.
For I delight in the law of God, in my inner being,
but I see in my members another law waging war against the law of my mind and making me captive to the law of sin that dwells in my members.
Wretched man that I am! Who will deliver me from this body of death?

Try this experiment:

Say to yourself "I will not (a negative) think about drugs (another negative)." Try this over the next hour.

What happened? You want to use drugs, correct?

THE ONLY WAY YOU CAN GET RID OF A NEGATIVE IN A HEALTHY WAY IS TO REPLACE IT WITH A POSITIVE. That is why diets don't work and willpower will never work in your deliverance from your addiction. You must walk in GRACE.
Do you identify with Paul? Write a brief account of one time in your addiction that the more you swore you wouldn't use again, the stronger seemed the urge to use:

How do you walk in grace? Well, turn to the next page.

GRACE IS AMAZING! It says that there is no longer any shame in falling short of the holiness of God.

Grace says that God Himself paid the price for us to be rightly related to Him. For that to happen, someone had to die! But not just anyone, it had to be someone perfect. Blood had to be paid to buy us back from satan. God the Son came in the likeness of us and walked a perfect life and paid His blood. Now the requirements have been paid once and for all.

Rom 8:1-4 There is therefore now no condemnation for those who are in Christ Jesus. For the law of the Spirit of life has set you free in Christ Jesus from the law of sin and death. For God has done what the law, weakened by the flesh, could not do. By sending his own Son in the likeness of sinful flesh and for sin, he condemned sin in the flesh, in order that the righteous requirement of the law might be fulfilled in us, who walk not according to the flesh but according to the Spirit.

There is one simple requirement. We must have our minds set on what He wants. If we will, He will deliver us as we follow Him. That is why you must become a 5 so He can be dominant in your life.

Rom 8:5-7 For those who live according to the flesh set their minds on the things of the flesh, but those who live according to the Spirit set their minds on the things of the Spirit. For to set the mind on the flesh is death, but to set the mind on the Spirit is life and peace. For the mind that is set on the flesh is hostile to God, for it does not submit to God's law; indeed, it cannot.

Grace says that God the Spirit is *not ashamed to live in us.* He no longer lives in a temple, in the Holy of Holies where men were struck dead if they were unclean in His presence. No, He now lives *in us.* If anyone did find the Arc of the Covenant it would be empty.

Because the Spirit lives *in* us, we have the power to be free! Not by our power, but by His. **He is not a "higher power," open for everyone's interpretation.** He is not above somewhere and you have to find the key to call Him down.

Rom 8:11 If the Spirit of him who raised Jesus from the dead dwells in you, he who raised Christ Jesus from the dead will also give life to your mortal bodies through his Spirit who dwells in you.
Romans 8:13-15 For if you live according to the flesh you will die, but if by the Spirit you put to death the deeds of the body, you will live.
For all who are led by the Spirit of God are sons of God.
For you did not receive the spirit of slavery to fall back into fear, but you have received the Spirit of adoption as sons, by whom we cry, "Abba! Father!"

As you, day by day, have your mind set on what His will is for that day or hour, you will find yourself walking in grace in the Spirit. You will overcome this addiction.

If you fall, remember, you are His child. He still loves you.

Rom 8:16-17 The Spirit himself bears witness with our spirit that we are children of God, and if children, then heirs—heirs of God and fellow heirs with Christ, provided we suffer with him in order that we may also be glorified with him.

BEFORE WE CONTINUE, you must be rightly related to God. What we are going to have you do in the rest of this manual *will not work* unless you are related to God. We must be sure of that. You cannot be right with God because your parents were. You can't be right with God because you were at one time as a child. You can't be right with God because you got goose bumps one time because you had a religious experience. No, there is a specific time that you submit to Him and ask Jesus to be your Savior as well as your Lord. As you have seen from Scripture, you should be water baptized as soon as possible.

To walk in grace, you must accept God's gift of grace. It involves *believing* what the Scripture has said about Jesus, simply accepting His grace, and confessing you have been separated from Him:

John 3:16-18 "For God so loved the world, that he gave his only Son, that whoever believes in him should not perish but have eternal life. For God did not send his Son into the world to condemn the world, but in order that the world might be saved through him. Whoever believes in him is not condemned, but whoever does not believe is condemned already, because he has not believed in the name of the only Son of God."

1 John 1:8-10 "If we say we have no sin, we deceive ourselves, and the truth is not in us. If we confess our sins, he is faithful and just to forgive us our sins and to cleanse us from all unrighteousness. If we say we have not sinned, we make him a liar, and his word is not in us."

Repeat this simple prayer aloud: "Father God, I believe that you love me just as I am. I confess I cannot run my life on my own, and I ask that you forgive me for trying. I confess that I have been separated from You and have sinned. I ask that you forgive me, and I invite You, Jesus, to come into my humble life and be my Savior and my Lord.

I will do my best to follow You day by day, one day at a time. I will do my best to look inward to your Spirit and thereby, have my mind set on what you want day by day.

If I fall, I will come to you immediately, and ask for your forgiveness and help. I cannot live without your grace." Amen

*Signed:*_____

*Date:*_____

Now, you are related to God. You are His child. Compared to Him, always remain a child.

You will never be perfect. He doesn't expect His children to be perfect. He wants you to mature and not remain a baby, but He doesn't expect you to be 21 years old when you are just starting to walk with Him. You have just been "born again". You are starting over.

We are now going to start a journey that will help you *completely* change how you see life and relate to yourself, others and God. Remember, we said freedom and any addiction will require you to change your addictive mindset and lifestyle.

STEP 3. HEALING THE ADDICTIVE ROOT

Drugs are not the problem. The problem is the lack of ease we have within ourselves that we have tried to anesthetize with drugs. That lack of ease is the "root" of our addiction. It is the source of the bad fruit in our lives. It does no good just to try to prune the branches if we want to get rid of our addiction. We have to pull up the root.

No one walks into a vineyard and says "oh, look at the roots!" They are hidden, deep underground. It is that way with our lack of ease. In fact, many of the roots of the things we are going to ask you to face may be so deeply buried that they may not come to the surface immediately. That is why it is important to remember what we talked about earlier about going through this manual more than once and continuing your commitment to the group.

How do you know there are still roots there? It's like the dandelions keep springing up in your lawn. You cut the grass and the dandelions, but if the roots are still there, they keep coming up again.

To remove the roots requires surgery. Sometimes it is painful, but the healing is worth it. **The addict's main problem is that he has been running from pain all his life. HE DOESN'T UNDERSTAND THAT HE CAN STOP AND FACE IT BECAUSE HE HAS SOMEONE GREATER THAN HIMSELF TO GIVE IT TO. We are not built to carry that pain inflicted on us by the sin of others--only Jesus Christ is.** You now have a real and new relationship with Him. You don't have to run from the pain anymore.

As an average person, you are a walking history book of personal wars and wounds. You have made vows and conclusions about life and the people around you. The battles with those who have hurt you are still going on within you. They cause you to be defensive and/or combative with those around you today. Many people have a hard time accepting what I just said. They see their life as a "straight line"--i.e., "What happened to me in my past couldn't possibly affect me today." This is especially true if you are one of those who have repressed your feelings. You were taught to "shake it off! Don't let it bother you." So you buried those things deep within you and thought they went away.

In many ways, your life is like the rings in a tree, or the layers of an onion. If you cut them open, you can see where there was a lean year or a fire. To look at that tree from the outside, you would never guess what was on the inside. But for humans, the analogy is not quite that simple. We don't just bury a hard winter within us and get on with life. If we don't allow those hurts to heal, they affect the rest of our life in indirect ways. This is true because of something called EMOTIONAL BRANCHING. Look at the diagram:

Notice that with the passing of time, the original emotion is replaced by another one. This will continue until the original hurt is dealt with. A person will tend to blame the current events and people for the predominant emotion he is feeling at the time, but the energy is being supplied by something that started long before that. Typically, he has lost touch with the original event and may even have difficulty bringing it to memory.

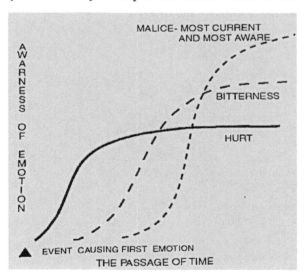

20

The roots of our addictions are deep within the "soil of our heart." The Bible used the term "heart" to explain the "inner man." In contemporary terms, it could accurately be called the "child within." It is the emotional center of our being. When you feel angry or sad, there is a definite feeling around the area of your heart. We have all experienced that feeling at times.

The Bible has much to say about the "heart" and its influence on addictions. It, too, says that it is where everything begins. Let's look at what Jesus has to say about it first:

Note that the SECRET of the kingdom of heaven was being given to the disciples.

Matt 13:10-12 Then the disciples came and said to him, "Why do you speak to them in parables?"
And he answered them, "To you it has been given to know **the secrets of the kingdom of heaven**, but to them it has not been given.
For to the one who has, more will be given, and he will have an abundance, but from the one who has not, even what he has will be taken away."

The REASON these people could not understand was because their "heart" had become dull (hard). If they would soften their heart, Jesus could heal them.

Who are these people who are not "getting it"? They are the people left over from the ministry of John the Baptist who came to prepare the way for Jesus.

Luke 1:17 "And he will go before Him in the spirit and power of Elijah, to turn the **hearts** of the fathers to the children, and the disobedient to the wisdom of the just, **to make ready for the Lord a people prepared**."

Many of the hard places of our hearts have to do with **family matters.**

Many people have areas of both softness and hardness in their hearts. These hard areas are the result of vows, wounds that have never healed, bitterness and so on.

Matt 13:13-22 "This is why I speak to them in parables, because seeing they do not see, and hearing they do not hear, nor do they understand.
Indeed, in their case the prophecy of Isaiah is fulfilled that says: 'You will indeed hear but never understand, and you will indeed see but never perceive.'"
For this people's **heart has grown dull**, and with their ears they can barely hear, and their eyes they have closed, lest they should see with their eyes and hear with their ears and understand with their heart and turn, **and I would heal them**.
But blessed are your eyes, for they see, and your ears, for they hear.
For truly, I say to you, many prophets and righteous people longed to see what you see, and did not see it, and to hear what you hear, and did not hear it.
"Hear then the parable of the sower:
When anyone hears the word of the kingdom and does not understand it, the evil one comes and snatches away what has been sown in his heart. This is what was sown along the path.
As for what was sown on rocky ground, this is the one who hears the word and immediately receives it with joy, yet he has no root in himself, but endures for a while, and when tribulation or persecution arises on account of the word, immediately he falls away.
As for what was sown among thorns, this is the one who hears the word, but the cares of the world and the deceitfulness of riches choke the word, and it proves unfruitful."

WHAT IS THE FRUIT?

The fruit is THE FRUIT OF THE HOLY SPIRIT. They are described in Gal 5:22 **love, joy, peace, patience, kindness, goodness, faithfulness, gentleness, and self-control.**

There is no "high" like the presence of the fruit of the Holy Spirit in your life. Your own natural neurotransmitters can do much more than any drug can do.[7] God has wired you to live this way, but mankind has been looking for other things. The fruit of the Holy Spirit is what every human being has been looking for.

Notice in Eph 4 passage that **the reason the people were separated from the life of God (the fruit of the Holy Spirit) was due to the** *hardening of their hearts.*

Because they had hardened their hearts, they **could not understand God's way of life** *and became addicted.*

Matt 13:23 As for what was sown on good soil, this is the one who hears the word and understands it. He indeed bears fruit and yields, in one case a hundredfold, in another sixty, and in another thirty.

Eph 4:17-21 Now this I say and testify in the Lord, that you must no longer walk as the Gentiles do, in the futility of their minds.

They are darkened in their understanding, alienated from the life of God because of the ignorance that is in them, due to their hardness of heart.

They have become callous and have given themselves up to sensuality, greedy to practice every kind of impurity.

But that is not the way you learned Christ!—

Assuming that you have heard about him and were taught in him, as the truth is in Jesus.

For healing to come, three distinct steps are to be taken:

1. Put off the old man

2. Be made new in the attitude of our minds

3. Then, we can put on the new man.

The Scripture shows us *that it is our responsibility* to put off the "old man."

For years, I thought Jesus was the farmer. I waited for Him to come and take out the rocks and thorns from my garden. We now understand that *we* are the farmer. We have been given another chance to tend our very own GARDEN OF EDEN. But now, the garden is in our heart. We are to *get rid of everything that impedes the growth of the fruit of the Holy Spirit.* If we will do that, the Holy Spirit will do the rest in our lives!

Well, then what kinds of things impede the growth of the fruit of the Holy Spirit?

Jesus was very clear about the worries of life and the deceitfulness of wealth in the parable of the sower. He was also clear about walking in sin. All of those things will keep the fullness of God from growing in your life.

But what about the **rocks**? What are they? Remember, they are hidden. There is a thin layer of soil, but underneath are rocks--hard places of the heart that keep God's word from growing the fruit in our emotions. The rocks are hard places of a heart that is otherwise soft. They are there as a result of living and learning to protect ourselves in a world that is cruel. That defense worked at one time, but as we grew older, the consequences affected our lives in dramatic ways.

It is like the military person: at the time, to survive he had to learn NOT TO FEEL because the enemy was all around him. He couldn't let down for a moment. He also could NOT TALK ABOUT FEELINGS because then he might drop his guard, and that would be dangerous. Last of all, he learned NOT TO TRUST, because it could be very dangerous for him. All of those survival techniques were very important at the time, but they didn't work when he came home from the war. All of us have had our own war time. The severity of our trauma varies and so does our response to that trauma. **But at any rate, when we decided, no matter how many years ago, not to feel, not to talk about our feelings or not to trust, it set us off down the addictive path.** All of us in this group have come to this point in our lives where we must look at the rocks in our hearts. They are causing so much inner turmoil.

A word of caution: There are many well-meaning people who say that what happened to them in their pasts could not possibly affect how they act today. I have had physicians in my counseling office who have said that, and yet when they got down to the base of their problem, there was always a root that started the whole thing. The reason for this mistake is that we have "numbed out" our inner feelings, and the memories that go with them, in order to survive. People who make this mistake don't want to talk about the past. They want to "move on," "get on with it," but I can tell you they are going nowhere until they drop the load of rocks they have been carrying around for years. Don't make that mistake!

Another word of caution has to do with blank areas of your memory. Of course, some of that can be because of burned-out brain cells after years of using drugs. But, sometimes it can be because of a history of sexual abuse or other trauma. If this is true of you, go slowly. You cannot and should not push it! God has given us the ability to cope with trauma by blocking it out at the time. It has to be healed, but at a pace you can handle. The memories come back at the rate you are able to progress, but you shouldn't try to go any faster than that. You may need one-on-one support if you start to have flashbacks because most people who experience this "healing crisis" need assurance and support during this time.

These rocks must be thrown out of our gardens, and we are going to walk you through the process. *They are what gave your "old self" its personality.* Therefore, if you want to be healed, they must be discarded.

REVIEW: Let's look at some truths from previous pages before we go on. Modern science has discovered what the Bible has said all along. Compare the biblical antidote from Eph 4 with the addictive progression from page 3.

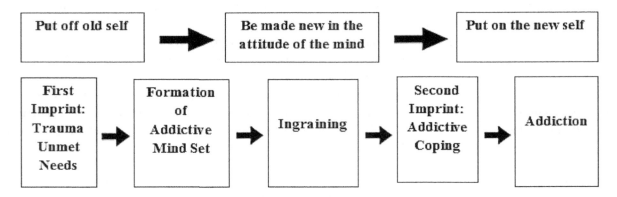

Put off old self	→	Be made new in the attitude of the mind	→	Put on the new self

First Imprint: Trauma Unmet Needs	→	Formation of Addictive Mind Set	→	Ingraining	→	Second Imprint: Addictive Coping	→	Addiction

Notice again, that the formation of the negative portions of your "old self" involves two areas:
Trauma and unmet needs. *It was in response to these negative influences that you formed your addictive mindset.* BUT IT IS HERE THAT ADDICTS SOMETIMES REMAIN IN THEIR STRONGEST DENIAL AND FAIL TO GAIN VICTORY OVER THE ROOT OF THEIR ADDICTION. It has to do with their love for their families or their yet undiscovered addiction to approval from their dysfunctional families that cause them to continue denying "that it was really that bad." They fail to understand or are ignorant of the concept of the "**blessing**" need that is deeply embedded in every human being.

Let's look at the elements of the **BLESSING** and compare it with a destructive environment.

Elements of the Blessing	Destructive Environment
1. Meaningful touch: hugs, kisses, hand on shoulder.	1. Slapping, punching; no touch; no hugs.
2. Words of value: You're a good kid. You really mean a lot to us.	2. Put downs; cruel words or generally negative response. Words like "stupid, lazy, fat, skinny."
3. Words of hope for your future: You are really going to be something someday. You are going to be the best…..	3. Discouragement of overstepping your "abilities." "Who do you think you are? You'll never amount to anything"
4. Commitment to your future: Always there for you; show up for support without running your life; purchase things what will help you.	4. Abandonment: Not there when you needed them the most. "You can do it kid! Figure it out!"

BLESSING MUST SUPERSEDE DISCIPLINE BY A RATIO OF SOMEWHERE AROUND 10 TO 1 TO GAIN A HEALTHY CONCEPT OF SELF! That seems to be the way God wired us. This little known fact is why many addicts will discount their past as being unhealthy. It really didn't seem that bad and besides, we've always been told that if you spare the rod, you'll spoil the child. But the truth is, I can say to you 3 times "You're really doing a good job." If on the very next time I say, "You're really doing a lousy job!" you will tend to not remember the 3 affirmations, but will dwell on and be consumed by the negative input. No, I have to affirm you about 9 straight times *before* I criticize you once for that criticism to have little or no effect of you. *This is why so many Americans don't see their families as being dysfunctional and remain in denial.*

I am amazed that many current authors are ignoring this in relation to addictions. They too have discounted its importance. YOU NEED THE BLESSING BEFORE YOU CAN DEVELOP A HEALTHY SELF IMAGE AS A CHILD. If you don't receive it from the most important people in your life, you will respond to them in a way that will form the addictive root and addictive mindset. That is why the fastest growing self-help group organization in America today is Adult Children of Alcoholics (ACOA). But, alcohol is not the problem in the home! It's that the family is dysfunctional--it's sick. In short, the parents don't know how to bless their children who grow up with the kinds of insecurities that drive them to anesthetize their pain. These families can be chaotic, angry or just cold--never touching or talking about feelings. But, whatever the scenario, the kids catch three things: DON'T FEEL, DON'T TALK ABOUT FEELINGS, AND DON'T TRUST. It is estimated that **80% of all Americans come from dysfunctional homes**, and that is a conservative figure. Look at the following comparison between the traits of an addictive personality and the 20 symptoms from being affected by growing up in a dysfunctional family.

Addictive Personality	20 Symptoms From Dysfunctional Family
-self obsessed -selfless – pseudo identity -inner emptiness -without meaning or purpose -approval addicted -hard on self -guilt ridden--** often repressed anger showing itself as guilt. As children, real self was squashed, as in stifling expression of anger or sex. Felt anger, but repressed it. Addiction gives reason to feel guilty and punish themselves. -angry -repression -numbness -inner tension -afraid to risk - hidden dependency on others -needs not met -trouble with authority figures -blame others -poor coping skills -wishful thinking -never grew up -no boundaries--let people cross them all the time -impulsive -cannot parent self -intimacy problems -cannot enjoy life or have fun[8]	-guess at what normal is -have difficulty following projects through from beginning to end -lie when it would be just as easy to tell the truth -judge self without mercy -have difficulty having fun -take self too seriously -have difficulty with intimate relationships -overreact to changes over which they have no control -feel different from other people -constantly seek approval and affirmation -either super-responsible or super-irresponsible -extremely loyal, even in the face of evidence that loyalty is not deserved. -look for immediate as opposed to deferred gratification -lock self into courses of action without considering other options or consequences of actions -seek tension and crisis and then complain about the results -fear rejection or abandonment, yet reject others -fear failure but sabotage success -fear criticism and judgment, yet criticize others -manage time poorly and don't set priorities that work well for them[9]

We have taken the time to explain these things to you to, hopefully, prevent you from brushing over this section lightly and to help you come out of you denial about these matters if that was the case.

Rocks: Identifying them.

1. Bitter roots: These are people or events that we hold in judgment. We have gone to bed on our anger about it for many months or years and the anger turned to a deep seeded malice towards those people or events. We hardened ourselves toward them.

2. Vows: These are areas of our heart that we have hardened in defense to prevent trauma from happening again. They cause us to be rigid. All or nothing words were used such as "never" as in "I will never let anyone tell me what to do again!" Often, there was a specific time you made the vow that you may have forgotten about, but at other times it may have been an attitude that gradually gained power in your life.

3. Wounds that haven't healed: The scar tissue around these wounds of the heart causes us to be fearful and defensive. We are still raw even though the incident may have happened years ago.

4. Generation curses: These are family traits that are in your family line, such things as an "Irish temper" or alcoholism. As you look at your parents and grandparents, you will see a history of negative traits that seem to be handed down from generation to generation.

5. Soul ties: This is a result of having sexual intercourse with people other than your husband or wife. The bible teaches that when you have sexual intercourse with any person, you are made one in spirit with them as well. This is why some people still fantasize about someone they had sex with before they were married and yet still love their mate.

6. Demonic harassment: When we hold things in our heart that are of the devil's territory, he can harass us. He stirs up the inner turmoil we have. We can never say, "The devil made me do it", but he sure can influence us to make us want to do it. It is important to understand that we have no authority over him in our own lives if we hold his territory. It's like having a secret agent in your camp from the enemy's side. He is there because *someone* is cooperating with him.

I know you are eager to begin, so let's get started cleaning our garden or as Evelyn prefers, your house. You may do this by yourself, but it is usually more effective if you have the leader of your group pray with you during this time.

STEPS TO MINISTERING HOUSE CLEANING

Step 1. Forgiveness and Bitter Roots.

Please fill out the following checklist. Place a mark along each entry you identify with:

___ I feel angry much of the time.

___ I avoid certain people.

___ I haven't spoken to certain people for a long time.

___ When I think of certain people in my past, I get mad.

___ I daydream about how I might get even sometimes.

___ I have a lot of negative memories.

___ I can't remember much about some of my history.

___ I don't like to talk about certain subjects. I get angry if I do.

___ I have secretly wished that some people would die.

___ I don't wish some people harm, but I don't wish them any good either.

All of the above show symptoms of unforgiveness. What is UNFORGIVENESS? A good definition is RETROSPECT ANGER AND/OR HURT. We call it "HARD FEELINGS."

Look at the list again. How many have to do with hard feelings? _____

FORGIVENESS has happened when you can sincerely wish someone good and not harm. It has happened when you can talk about a person or the past without hard feelings. It doesn't mean you won't have butterflies in your stomach the next time you meet that person. It *does* mean you will relate to them in the NOW and not out of the past.

UNFORGIVENESS IS A SIN. You must face that today. It is a sin because: 1. It is a barrier between you and God, 2. It damages you, and 3. It damages others.

Education regarding forgiveness: Forgiveness is not as simple as some people make it. You can see that by the fact that many people go through the motions of forgiveness, but still have hard feelings. Sometimes they feel that they have done all they can do or rationalize their bitterness away.

Forgiveness comes in two stages:

1. The legal transaction: **You must have someone bigger than you carry the sins of others**. Jesus Christ came to carry the sin of all. You are not big enough to carry them. If you try it will kill you. There is a time when you need to transfer the sins of others from your account to God's account--they owe Him now.

2. The emotional transformation: The legal transaction doesn't automatically make the hard feelings go away. Your emotions change as you continue to release those people **every time you feel hard feelings rising up against them**. YOU OVERCOME AN EMOTION WITH A **BELIEF**, not another emotion. When you feel the emotion, you point to the time you **believe** you transferred those people to the only One who can take their sin.

Read these scriptures:

Matt. 6:9-14, Luke 11:2-4. Note that you are *in bondage* if you hold others in bondage by unforgiveness.

Matt. 6:14-15 Jesus EMPHASIZED THEIR SINS, not persons. You can love people, but hate their sin. Sin makes people do things. Think about it--how does that help?

Luke 6:33-37 You have been crucifying yourself. Jesus paid the price to judge and condemn on Judgment Day. If you want to judge and condemn, then the consequences of taking someone's sin upon yourself causes *you* great pain. Payday will come! You can afford to release people to someone greater.

Luke 17:1-10 Go to those against whom you have hard feelings, **if at all possible**. Sometimes, this is the only way to have a release in your life. **Sometimes this is not possible; it would damage *them*.** An example would be your parents, who may be so dysfunctional that you couldn't confront them. Or another example would be if you are a sexually abused woman and the attacker was your father. You may not be able to go to them at first, or ever. But we are talking about the LEGAL TRANSACTION of releasing these people to God's debt from ours. He transferred those debts from your account to His when He wrote the check in His blood. He paid for the sins of your attackers. Let Him take them. Let's look at what Jesus says here:

1. vs. 1-3   If you don't extend forgiveness to the weak ones in your life, you can cause them to sin.

2. vs. 3-4   GO TO THEM. Don't let the sun go down on your anger. If they repent, forgive them. Don't hold grudges after that.

3. vs. 5-10   Forgiveness has nothing to do with faith. It is an act of obedience so that God can work in that person's life as well your own.

Matt. 5:44-48 PRAY FOR THOSE WHO DON'T REPENT. The word "perfect" is "telios" in the original language Jesus spoke here. It carries with it the process of being made complete. As you pray *consistently* for God to bless those who *won't repent* of wrongdoing in your life, you are completed. YOU WILL FIND THAT YOUR HARD FEELINGS TOWARD THEM START TO SOFTEN. This is a supernatural thing. I've personally seen a number of people be transformed as they do this. Remember, this only works on those who won't repent. If you are supposed to go to them because God knows they will repent if you approach them in the right way, then prayer alone will not be effective.

WARNING:

It is not uncommon for people to come to an incident from their history that is hard to give up. You may come to something and be tempted to skip over it, ignore it, or be insincere in ridding yourself of it. I can tell you though, that there will be no freedom unless you handle it. Here are some common obstacles:

A. NO JUSTICE FACTOR The attitude is, "If I don't hold this person accountable, who will?" An example would be someone who has been purposely cruel to you and gotten away with it. "Vengeance is mine, I will repay, says the Lord." (Rom. 12:19 ESV) You can be sure that God deals with these people. They can pay Him now or pay Him later, but payday always comes.

B. POWER Holding anger inside can give a person a false sense of power. It feels like you are in control, especially when you growl and people scurry around or stay out of your way. The bitterness is controlling no one but you. If you think about it there is no one who actually does what you want them to do. Behind your back, they will do what they are going to do anyway. Therefore, you have never been in control and bitterness is poisoning everyone around you.

C. TOO PAINFUL An example would be a sexually abused woman or a veteran. Those who have horrifying memories feel like they will go off the deep end if they bring some of those memories to the surface. If this is you, don't fear; take your time. When you face it, you will become very emotional, but you won't lose control. When you are ready to face it, it will come to the surface--allow it to. Have someone you know and trust and who cares about you present when you are ready. Tell them to take your hand quietly and put their arm around you. They don't have to speak.

D. LOSS OF SYMPATHY This is called "sweet pain." You don't have to use negative circumstances to gain people's attention. You have good merits. Quit feeling sorry for yourself. It may be why you don't have as many friends as you would like. You drain them with your negativism when you are around them. Let go of it.

Go back to page 7 and look closely at the compulsion spiral in this booklet. Notice how blaming others for our emotional hurt keep us from dealing with ourselves. It keeps us in repression, which is the same thing as denial.

Blame is another way of describing the debt we hold over people who have hurt us. We go over and over hurtful episodes in our minds as if they happened yesterday. THERE IS ONLY ONE WAY TO BREAK FREE FROM THIS TRAP. IT IS TO RELEASE THESE PEOPLE FROM OUR DEBT INTO GOD'S DEBT. That is the essence of forgiveness.

Forgiveness is for US, not the people who have hurt us! It releases us from the past. If we don't release, we CRUCIFY OURSLEVES. Oh, we don't have nail prints in our hands and feet, but we do in our hearts.

Jesus Christ is the ONLY one who can give us true relief! You see, He paid the price to judge and condemn on the last day. He paid His dues. He suffered for us and yet did not sin. Only the perfect can judge the imperfect. Everyone will face Him and every knee will bow to Him. He was God Himself. He took on human form, and came and walked among us for a while to identify with our hurts and weaknesses. He took ALL of our sorrows and diseases upon Himself.

He will not only take care of those who haven't repented on the last day, but also will work in their lives in the here and now to bring them to repentance.

If we hold people in our judgment and condemnation, Jesus says to us, "OK You go to the cross. If you want to do my job, you will have to pay the price as I did." And we do. The price we pay for being God in someone else's life comes out in ulcer, arthritis, heart disease and inner turmoil. We remove ourselves from benefits of God's family. Take, for instance, a family at the dinner table. The son sasses his mother, so the father sends him to his room to think things over. He can come back only if he is sorry and will ask forgiveness. He is still a member of the family, but is not getting the benefits. He can stay in his room and sulk, lick his wounds, and be hungry all night, OR he can think it over, go back and apologize to his mother and eat dessert. As soon as we pray and release people from the bondage we've held them in, we are released and forgiven by the Lord and our benefits are restored. Many times people receive healing (physical as well as emotional) the moment they do this.

Bitter root judgments:

Heb 12:15 "See to it that no one fails to obtain the grace of God; that no "root of bitterness" springs up and causes trouble, and by it many become defiled."

Matt 7:1 "Judge not, that you be not judged." For with the judgment you pronounce you will be judged, and with the measure you use it will be measured to you.

Gal 6:7 "Do not be deceived: God is not mocked, for whatever one sows, that will he also reap."

Bitterness comes in stages as we saw in the diagram of emotional branching earlier on page 20.

1. Hurt   4. Anger
2. Disappointment   5. Hate
3. Resentment   6. Revenge--the root has formed.

Some bitter root judgments will cause us to judge people for how they act and appear and then expect others or ourselves **never** to be that way, like Evelyn's judgment of her father and mother. We are so surprised to find out we are just like them.

Author John Sanford tells about a young man who judged his mother, who had grown fat and sloppy. She kept a dirty house, which repulsed him, so he judged her. His wife before he married her never could please her father and she judged him. All went well after they were married, until she became pregnant. After the baby came, she didn't lose her excess weight. Her husband became critical and upset just as her father used to do. Consequently, she became insecure and started to eat more and became just like his mother. They were caught in a trap and found themselves powerless to escape.[10]

The Law of Judgment that says, "the measure we mete out is the measure we must receive" had taken effect in the couple's life. Even if our judgments are true about a parent, if we judge them harshly, the law of Deut. 5:16 concerning honoring our parents goes into effect and ensures that in whatever regard we are harshly judging our parents, life will not go well with us. Our judgment was a seed sown which by law must someday be repaid.

But what if my parent sexually or physically abused me? Does honoring them mean I have to say that is OK? No, not at all. *Honor does not mean we ignore sin against us, even if it is our parents*. Honor means "to give them weight" in your life. Don't disregard them and count them as nothing. If they gave you nothing else, they gave you life! If you think about it, there were also some good times. The emphasis is *bitter* judgment. God doesn't command us not to judge. He commands us to not be the avenger and condemner in people's lives especially when we are doing the same thing. There has been confusion about this but there really is no confusion in the Scripture. Let's take a moment to look at this important issue, because if we interpret what He has said to mean that we are to ignore sin against us no matter what, then God simply becomes another dysfunctional parent telling us not to feel.

Matt 7:3-5 "Why do you see the speck that is in your brother's eye, but do not notice the log that is in your own eye? Or how can you say to your brother, 'Let me take the speck out of your eye,' when there is the log in your own eye? You hypocrite, first take the log out of your own eye, and then you will see clearly to take the speck out of your brother's eye."

> The emphasis in this passage of Jesus' comments on the subject is twofold: hypocrisy and the sawdust and the plank. They are of the same nature. A hypocrite is someone who judges another for the very thing he is doing. Sawdust is of the same material as the plank. Jesus is warning us not to judge someone for the same thing you do.

Matt 18:15 "If your brother sins against you, go and tell him his fault, between you and him alone. If he listens to you, you have gained your brother."

Luke 17:3 "Pay attention to yourselves! If your brother sins, rebuke him, and if he repents, forgive him."

> The two scriptures taught by Jesus, clearly involve judgment. But the judgment is not harsh. It has restoration in mind.

I Cor 5:9-12 I wrote to you in my letter not to associate with sexually immoral people not at all meaning the sexually immoral of this world, or the greedy and swindlers, or idolaters, since then you would need to go out of the world. But now I am writing to you not to associate with anyone who bears the name of brother if he is guilty of sexual immorality or greed, or is an idolater, reviler, drunkard, or swindler—not even to eat with such a one. For what have I to do with judging outsiders? Is it not those inside the church whom you are to judge?

I Cor 6:3 Do you not know that we are to judge angels? How much more, then, matters pertaining to this life!

Bitter seeds sown always produce a crop. Have you ever noticed how many seeds are in a cantaloupe? A small seed of resentment, anger or revenge held against a family member, even from childhood, may be sown and forgotten, but the longer it remains undetected or neglected, the larger it grows.

The Good News is that the full legal penalty of sowing and reaping was fulfilled upon the body of our Lord Jesus in the pain of the cross. We still have our part to do; the cross is not automatic. *We must give the sin of others against us to someone who is built to carry it. We are not built to carry the sin of others. We end up crucifying ourselves*. Therefore, let's begin the process now:

Take a piece of paper (Work Sheet A in the Appendix) and list names of people who have hurt you and people you have hurt.

Read this prayer out loud:

Dear Heavenly Father, I come to you in Jesus' Name, asking you to forgive me for holding grudges. I am sorry for the way I have acted and rededicate my life to you today.

I ask you come into my heart afresh today. Please forgive me for not living for you as I should have. I receive you afresh as my Savior, Healer and Deliverer. I crown you King and Lord over every part of my life. I will live for You to the best of my ability from now on. Thank You for Your love and mercy. I renounce satan and his demons: they no longer have a hold on me. I am under the blood of Jesus--HE IS MY LORD.

Today I choose to release the people on this list, not because I "feel" forgiveness or because they are right, but because I choose to be obedient to you, Father. I realize your ways are higher than my ways, and today I release them from my hurt, my disappointment, my resentment, my anger, my hate, my unforgiveness and my bitterness, especially my parents and family, or anyone that I have made bitter-root judgments against. I release them from my judgment and plow up the ground where the bad seeds were sown, turn under those bitter roots, and plant new seeds of love, acceptance and forgiveness.

I thank You that I can bind satan and break the hold he had on me in regard to this matter and break his power over my life. I make null and void all things I've reaped from the past. As I bind him according to Matthew 18:18, I know what I bind on earth has already been bound by you in heaven, and I command him to leave, in the Mighty Name of Jesus! Do not return. And now loose the spirit of love and the compassion of Jesus and the Spirit of Truth in my life to set me FREE!

Thank You, Lord. I will no longer reap from those bitter roots that I have sowed. Please have those I have hurt release me also, Lord. However, if you have anyone you specifically want me to contact I will do it. Just bring them to my remembrance.

Tear up the paper and put it in the wastebasket. Cup your hands in front of you and say to the Lord:

Lord Jesus, here are the people I have hurt and the ones who have hurt me. I release them to you. I pray for those who have despitefully used me. I pray for my enemies as you have commanded and ask You to bless them and save them. You say to give you my problems because you care for me. Thank You Lord. These people are no longer my problem; they are Yours! (Throw up your hands to God and let them go!) Thank you, Lord, for setting me free. Please heal me of my hurts in regard to these people. Please change my heart about them as only you can do!

Father God, I now release You of the things I have held against You. I've been wrong, and I'm sorry. I know you are a loving, caring Father, and I am grateful for Your forgiveness. Because You have forgiven and released me, I can and do forgive myself! Hallelujah!

You may shed some tears during this time. It is quite common and natural to do so. They are tears of relief. You *finally* have transferred a debt from your account to the only One who can pay. From now on, turn to him when you are upset instead to the memories of people who have wronged you.

Step 2. Inner healing of wounds: Turn to work sheet B in the Appendix and prayerfully fill in the following:

1. Age incident happened, i.e., 5 years old

2. Feeling when it occurred, i.e., fear; couldn't sleep for weeks.

3. Brief note on what happened, i.e., father slapped me in the face in front of my friends and said I was stupid.

Remember, the people who caused the hurts are in the hands of the Lord: it is time to face the problems they caused and get them healed. Otherwise, they will fester and open doors for those feelings to return.

God's Word refers many times to the wounded heart or wounded spirit. At times, the terms are interchangeable and at other times they are distinct. At any rate, the wounded heart or wounded spirit is a result of growing up, often in a dysfunctional home. We often *did not* receive the blessing we needed to develop healthy self-esteem. Instead, many of us suffered wounds *from people who loved us*. That made it even harder to deal with, because as children we have very naïve beliefs about life. We didn't understand at the time that mom and dad were not perfect and had their own set of wounds that caused them to lash out at times. That did not change the fact, though, that it *did* wound us and it *did* affect us. It is an area of our "heart" that needs to be softened, and thereby, healed.

God refers to our heart or spirit as capable of holding sin, not in the Holy Spirit, but in our human spirit.

Psalms 32:2 "Blessed is the man against whom the LORD counts no iniquity, and in whose spirit there is no deceit."

Psalms 51:10-12 "Create in me a clean heart, O God, and renew a right spirit within me. Cast me not away from your presence, and take not your Holy Spirit from me. Restore to me the joy of your salvation and uphold me with a willing spirit." (There is no need for a new spirit if nothing is wrong with the old one.)

Ezek 36:26 "And I will give you a new heart, and a new spirit I will put within you. And I will remove the heart of stone from your flesh and give you a heart of flesh."

Ezek 11:19 I will give them an undivided heart and put a new spirit in them; I will remove from them their heart of stone and give them a heart of flesh.

First, the Father wants to put a new spirit, a right spirit within us. Later He wants to renew us with His spirit, the Holy Spirit. But first, He wants us to clean house, so that there is no blockage--no encumbrances to what He wants to do in us.

II Cor 7:1 "Since we have these promises, beloved, let us cleanse ourselves from every defilement of body and spirit, bringing holiness to completion in the fear of God."

We are spending the time in Scripture on this subject so that you can see that God is concerned about those things that hold you back from the growth you really want. But some of you may *still* be struggling with believing that events early in our childhood could have a profound effect on us now, and that our spirit and/or heart has a large part to play in it.

Psalms 58:3 "The wicked are estranged from the womb; they go astray from birth, speaking lies."

James 2:26 "For as the body apart from the spirit is dead, so also faith apart from works is dead."

Job 32:8 "But it is the spirit in man, the breath of the Almighty, that makes him understand."

So we know that we have understanding in our spirits--not just in our minds. The following scripture refer to these truths:

Troubled	John 13:21 After saying these things, Jesus was troubled in his spirit, and testified, "Truly, truly, I say to you, one of you will betray me."
Fear	II Tim 1:7 "For God gave us a spirit not of fear but of power and love and self-control."

Testify	Romans 8:16-17 "The Spirit himself bears witness with our spirit that we are children of God, and if children, then heirs--heirs of God and fellow heirs with Christ, provided we suffer with him in order that we may also be glorified with him."
Longing	Isaiah 26:9 "My soul yearns for you in the night; my spirit within me earnestly seeks you. For when your judgments are in the earth, the inhabitants of the world learn righteousness."
Prayer	I Cor 14:14 "For if I pray in a tongue, my spirit prays but my mind is unfruitful."
Song	I Cor 14:15 "What am I to do? I will pray with my spirit, but I will pray with my mind also; I will sing praise with my spirit, but I will sing with my mind also."
Praise	I Cor 14:16 "Otherwise, if you give thanks with your spirit, how can anyone in the position of an outsider say 'Amen' to your thanksgiving when he does not know what you are saying?"
Envy	James 4:5 "Or do you suppose it is to no purpose that the Scripture says, 'He yearns jealously over the spirit that he has made to dwell in us?'"
Unfaithfulness	Psalms 78:8 "And that they should not be like their fathers, a stubborn and rebellious generation, a generation whose heart was not steadfast, whose spirit was not faithful to God"
Worship	John 4:23-24 "But the hour is coming, and is now here, when the true worshipers will worship the Father in spirit and truth, for the Father is seeking such people to worship him. God is spirit, and those who worship him must worship in spirit and truth."

John the Baptist leapt in Elizabeth's womb when Mary came to visit her in Luke 1:44. He was alive in his spirit; there was understanding in his spirit; he perceived and he leapt for joy--he reacted to what he perceived in the womb. During pregnancy in those days, mothers went aside, rested, studied and even read scriptures to the baby in the womb, praying for their perfect formation and so on. No wonder Jesus confounded the professors at the age of twelve--He was educated in the womb of spiritual things.

Our point is that even before birth, there can be things formed deeply within you. If after birth, life deals you some blows, those wounds can lie festering until they erupt in ways you have not understood until now. They can have a great deal to do with your addiction.

Such things as:

Rejection from our parents: Not so much from what was said or done, but a prevailing attitude that you caught that said "you are not important to us."

Lack of Love: As you go back and look at the elements of the blessing again, you may recognize you were not touched, hugged or told of your value. It was something you craved but didn't know if you had the right to ask for or expect.

Broken Heart: Many people are still grieving over the loss of a child hood they always wanted but never got. There is sometimes a relationship that you wanted so much, but ended up getting rejected and wounded as it fell apart. It broke your heart but you tried to pick up the pieces and get on with life.

Wounds growing up: Kids can be cruel. Some of our deepest wounds come from brothers or sister or kids in school.

Dr. Thomas Verney in his book, *The Secret Life of the Unborn Child*, relates, "There is no doubt that the child, while in the womb, hears, feels, and experiences what is going on in the environment of the mother. He learns, he makes reactions to what he is learning and he comes out of the womb already predisposed to interpret life according to what he experienced in the womb." Things such as character, personality and attitudes about "self" can start in the womb. He goes on to say, "It isn't just these strong emotions like love and hate that the child will experience, but it's emotions like ambivalence, and for example, like when the parents say, 'Oh no-- I'm pregnant! There is no way we want this child.', and then swing to the other side and say, 'Well of course we'll love this child, but how on earth are we going to care for this child" But, we'll make it somehow.' That kind of alternation affects the child and it will come out of the womb with a kind of lethargic personality." [11]

Paula Sandford, in one of her books, tells of one of their daughters that had a sleepy attitude--not really interested in anything. She was a sweet girl, but had no drive. Once they realized the problem, they prayed with her and asked her and asked the Lord to heal the wounding she had experienced because of *their* attitudes while carrying her. They had been anxious because of the possibilities of miscarriage, and therefore were ambivalent when they first learned she was on the way. Their daughter grew up to be a dynamic young lady after they prayed.[12]

Many researchers agree today that a negative attitude in mothers during pregnancy can be damaging to the unborn child. Miscarriage increases, and negative personality traits are seen in the child early in life.

Loud noises and music affect the unborn child. Some of the classical music such as passages by Mozart have a positive effect on the fetus but, loud music from Beethoven or rock music will cause the fetus to become restless. Many mothers have told researchers that they have had to leave rock concerts when the music becomes loud because the babies become so active that they cause her pain. After they find a quiet place, the baby settles down.

As we grow up, much happens to us as Evelyn relates. "A girl made fun of a dress my mother made me in the first grade". That incident changed my whole personality. I became an extrovert to prove I was somebody. Later in life, the enemy used this same person to hurt me even deeper. From there came rejection, hurt, anger, bitterness, unforgiveness and rebellion against all men and suspicion against women. Like a snowball rolling down a hill, I gathered more hurt and pain around me and it grew until it affected every part of my life." Issues like sexual abuse, physical and emotional abuse *have to be dealt with*. **Old things cannot pass away and all things cannot become new until old things are healed and forgiven**. As long as the sliver is in the sore, it will continue to fester.

You need to ask Jesus to walk back with you and heal you once and for all. If you are wondering about your children and your attitudes before they were born, do this: After you have received healing, share with them what you have learned. Ask them to pray with you a simple prayer of forgiveness and healing for them that you will find after our next prayer. Also, lead them through the prayer breaking generational curses.

Pray this prayer out loud:

Dear Heavenly Father, thank you for your tender mercies. Thank you for Jesus, as I come to you in his precious name, Father, I believe I've been wounded in my spirit from the womb, and right now I want it to go on record that I forgive my parents for this, because they had no more idea than I did how much the unborn child is alive and aware. I ask you now to forgive me for my lack of knowledge and release me from my anguish as I release my parents (living or dead). Heal my children as you are healing me, and I will be obedient to share with them what I have learned. Lord Jesus, I am asking you to identify with me in my hurts of rejection. You experienced rejection in a hideous way and can understand my pain. Heal my wounds of rejection, hopelessness, inadequacies, craving for love and even the effects of the turmoil my parents were going through that filled me with anxieties and fears from birth.

Come in Lord Jesus, and close those wounds, filling them with the healing balm of your Holy Spirit.

Now satan, I rebuke you from my past, up to the present, and I bind you and all your evil spirits that were assigned to me and mine, according to Matthew 18:18, commanding you to Go, Go, GO in Jesus' name. I break your power and recover myself out of the snare of the devil, and I loose ministering angels to come fill me with the love of God. Holy Spirit, fill me to overflowing with your spirit of God, a humble and contrite spirit, the unspeakable "Joy of the Lord," the garment of praise for the spirit of heaviness, the oil of gladness, and loving, forgiving, compassion for each other in Jesus. Thank you for healing me and setting me free, Jesus!"

Here is a prayer for your children. Meet with them if possible but if not, call them on the phone. Ask them to forgive you. You might say it like this:

"Will you forgive us for not wanting you when we first heard the news? We loved you when you came, and long before you were born we changed our feelings, but we want you to forgive us our ignorance of how it may have affected your life."

Ask God to speak deeply within their spirits and say: ***"My child, you are not a mistake. You have the right to be. We want you, we love you, and we thank You, Father for the gift of_____(child's name)! Thank You, Father, for their lives and the privilege of being their parents. We speak healing to their wounded spirits in Jesus' name."***

Step 3: Breaking of Unhealthy Vows:

We have mentioned vows before in our diagnosis of inner turmoil. Vows will make you take on a "bunker mentality". They will cause you to become very rigid and dig in. People will become threats to you for reasons you don't understand. Often, these vows are made early in life and men and women form their life around them. Jesus warned us about them:

Matt 5:33-37 "Again you have heard that it was said to those of old, 'You shall not swear falsely, but shall perform to the Lord what you have sworn.' But I say to you, 'Do not take an oath at all, either by heaven, for it is the throne of God, or by the earth, for it is his footstool, or by Jerusalem, for it is the city of the great King. And do not take an oath by your head, for you cannot make one hair white or black. Let what you say be simply 'Yes' or 'No'; anything more than this comes from evil.'" (ESV)

James 5:12 "But above all, my brothers, do not swear, either by heaven or by earth or by any other oath, but let your 'yes' be yes and your 'no' be no, so that you may not fall under condemnation."(ESV)

Jesus says anything beyond "yes or "no" is from the evil one. Why? **Vows will addict you**. They trap you and keep you in patterns you cannot break out of unless you break the back of the vow itself.

When I (Theo) was a young man, I was very hostile. I would fight at the drop of a hat. I often didn't want to fight, but when someone tried to tell me what to do, or force me to do something I didn't want to do I found this rage rising up in me. The only way I knew to relieve it was to set the other person straight--and I did.

After, I was married the same rage would rise up in me when I felt like my wife was trying to tell me what to do. It caused huge problems in our marriage, but like Adam I blamed my rage on my wife. I blamed her so often; I actually started *believing* she was causing it. We were married 10 years when my wife and I accepted Jesus into our lives. I was a heavy drinker and still, full of rage. Twenty years after we were married, I entered the ministry. I wasn't a drinker anymore but I still battled bouts with rage from time to time--especially if it had to do with my wife.

I had been a pastor for a year when my wife and I were driving home from a convention in New Mexico outside of Tucson Arizona, I went into one of my rages over something I felt my wife had done, but for the *first time I came out of my denial* and admitted to her and God that it wasn't her, but me. As we were unpacking in our motel room, I told her that I had been an angry man for a long time and I was tired of it. As I started recanting every incident in my life I could remember that had caused me a great deal of anger, she tried to stop me because she thought it was unhealthy. But, I knew something was going on. It was like playing an old record album or tape--I couldn't tell you the names of all the songs but, before one song was over I could start humming the next one. It was like that. I remembered things I thought I had completely forgotten about.

When I had reached about 14 years of age in my memory, I heard the Lord speak to my heart. If you are a new Christian I don't know how to explain His voice to you except to say He sounds like your inner voice but, there is revelation, power and you never forget it. I heard Him say, "The issue isn't how long you've been angry. The issue is how long you have been angry at women." At that moment, I saw things with a new light.

I saw the truth. Somewhere around 12 years of age I had made a vow. I can't remember actually writing it down or even talking to anyone about it--it was an attitude. The vow was, "No woman will ever control me again!" It was made in response to my mother and older sister. When my wife would *do anything* that triggered my fear of being controlled by women, I would blast her from my bunker--I had to be in control. That vow had almost caused us to divorce.

The power of unhealthy vows must be broken to be free from your addiction. We often look at them as a monument to our ego. We take pride in "being a man of my word" or having people admire us because we almost killed ourselves doing something we said we would do. But they keep us in our own prison with rigid bars holding us to "our word". Jesus warns us not to do that.

As addicts, vows have been one of our worst enemies. ***They are hidden in the framework of "willpower"***. At first, we made a vow every time we went back to our drug of choice not to use again and every time we fell we became more and more rigid. Our self-esteem hit the bottom and skidded into the addiction spiral with new energy. We couldn't see it then, but we do now.

If you have made vows in your history, they will be surrounded by words like "never", and "always". These are black and white words. They are promises to yourself to be completely in control in that area. They cause you to try to be omnipotent and must be identified. If not identified, you will continue to live by them.

In the space below, list your vows:

State the Vow	What Happened?

Pray this prayer out loud:

Heavenly Father, I come to you and ask your forgiveness for swearing I would not allow these things to happen in my life again. These vows have caused me to control others and myself in areas I have no power to do anything about. I come to you now and submit to You again. I ask that Your kingdom come and Your will be done in my life. I demolish and smash the power of these words spoken in ignorance earlier in my life. In the Name of Jesus Christ, I renounce them, turn from them and recognize them for what they are-- lies from the evil one. Lord I ask that you open my heart now to your truth. Give my heart the spirit of revelation to see your kingdom in fresh ways. Fill me with Your truth now, in Jesus Name. Thank you."

Step 4: Spiritual Housecleaning:

This step takes the least amount of time of all. In fact, 15-30 minutes; **but do not underestimate** the effectiveness of it. When you come to the point of being fed up and desperate because of drugs, and are ready to serve the Lord Jesus Christ, and "you are willing to" go through the previous steps we have discussed, including this one, there is a weight that will be lifted from your soul that will cause you to feel light--free. Most of the time, it is miraculous!

To believe in this modern time that Christians cannot be influenced by demons is to be ignorant of the ministry of the Lord Jesus Christ.

He came to:
>1. Preach the good news
>2. To heal the broken hearted.
>3. To proclaim freedom to the prisoners.
>4. To release the oppressed.
>> See Luke 4:18 and Isaiah 61:1-2.

There are three spirits that influence man:
>1. The Holy Spirit of God--The Good Spirit.
>2. Evil spirits (strongmen)--from satan.
>3. The human spirit--this can be influenced either way.

When ministering at the "Hotel", God's Holy Spirit would show me the strongholds satan would get over people to hold them in bondage. There are a number of strongmen listed in the Bible, such as:

spirit of fear--most common.
spirit of jealousy--(anger, hate, bitterness, etc.)
lying spirit
spirit of divination and familiar spirit
perverse and unclean spirits—perverted sex, homosexuality, etc…
spirit of haughtiness (pride) unforgiveness
spirit of heaviness (depression)
spirit of whoredoms
spirit of infirmity
dumb and deaf spirit
spirit of bondage (drugs and alcohol)
seducing spirit
spirit of error
spirit of anti-Christ
spirit of death and self-destruction (suicidal)

The most common spirits are those of fear, jealousy, haughtiness and bondage. We are not saying that these spirits "made me do it", but they sure can influence you in a strong way. When you hold the addictive root inside of you and have the addictive mind set, they have tremendous influence in your life. You will find that you will have your mind set on what they want instead of what the Holy Spirit wants (Romans 8:5) and have no self-control.

Martin Luther's definition of a "saint" was that he or she is a *realist. Reality is that there is a fourth dimension.* It is amazing to us how many Christians believe in the Holy Spirit of God, yet stick their heads in the sand and pretend like demonic spirits don't exist. To be a Christian and believe you are not in a battle with the forces of hell is not only stupid but dangerous. It's like being in Saigon during the Vietnam War and pretending like the enemy is far away in North Vietnam. As anyone who was there can tell you, that attitude killed many of our men. The enemy fights a Guerilla war. He is crafty. He isn't so stupid as to show his hand. He doesn't want us to know his devises. Yet God is clear on this subject. He commands us to be aware:

1 Pet 5:8 "Be sober-minded; be watchful. Your adversary the devil prowls around like a roaring lion, seeking someone to devour."

For you to be free from chemicals, *you must understand that it is not only a physical and emotional addiction you battle, but a spiritual addiction as well. There is a demonic force that helps drive your addiction. It must be dealt with.* Those who are not related to God, cannot see this. Yet in our Freedom Now Group, we have scores of people who have been set free from these influences and are walking in freedom. You are free to talk to them. The leader will give you their names. Just the same, many do not believe what we are saying about this influence and there is a reason:

1 Cor 2:11-14 "For who knows a person's thoughts except the spirit of that person, which is in him? So also no one comprehends the thoughts of God except the Spirit of God. Now we have received not the spirit of the world, but the Spirit who is from God, that we might understand the things freely given us by God. And we impart this in words not taught by human wisdom but taught by the Spirit, interpreting spiritual truths to those who are spiritual. The natural person does not accept the things of the Spirit of God, for they are folly to him, and he is not able to understand them because they are spiritually discerned."

We are constantly exposed to the spirit realm. Yet, if we love God, and are not walking in sin, *we have no need to fear transference or possession.* As Christians, we cannot be possessed because we belong to God. Possession implies ownership.

We need to stop now and discuss this very important theological truth, because many sincere Christians think that believers cannot be influenced by demons. This confusion comes from an unfortunate mistranslation in King James Bible. There is no such thing as "demon possessed" in the original language of the Bible. The word used is "diamonizomai", and means influence, NOT POSSESSION. A Christian cannot be possessed, because that implies ownership and we belong to the Father. Possession of the unsaved is not common, and if it happens, it is only temporarily when the spirit seizes the person. However, a Christian can be "energized" if he holds something that belongs to the devil's kingdom. When we remove those things from our lives, he loses his foothold.

Since the natural man does not understand the things of God, it follows that the natural man will not understand the things of satan. If the spiritual man understands the things of God, according to the above scripture, he also should understand the things of the spirit of the devil. **But,** here is the problem: although many Christians are instructed on the workings of the Holy Spirit, they are usually ignorant on the things **of the unholy spirit.** In America's victory in Desert Storm, much effort was spent in understanding Saddam Hussein's position and his tactics. When the allied forces struck, he didn't have a chance. It's supposed to be that way in the church.

Some churches will say, "I give all my time and thought to the Lord. I have no time or interest in the workings of satan." That sounds good, honorable and spiritual, but unfortunately it is unrealistic. We need to be aware of the devil's schemes, but at the same time, not preoccupied with them. Our focus is to be on the Lord and His business, with our hand on the sword and protected by our armor.

After you become clean and new creatures in Christ, you will be instructed on how to stay clean and safe, because God equips us for every problem if we'll apply ourselves to His instructions. Unless we have the Spirit of God dwelling in us, we will not grasp this subject. **All Christians should ask the Holy Spirit to give them understanding.** This is very important. The enemy will do everything possible to keep this truth from us, because our ignorance is the weapon he uses to bring disarray, confusion and destruction to the children of God. He has repeatedly brought division and confusion by using strong personal ties among the disorganized. He is using the spirit of rebellion to bring splits, splinter groups, cults and doctrines and disarray to God's people. Strong willed people have imposed their spirit upon the submissive and led them captive to spiritual slaughter. But, praise the Lord, we have been given weapons to bind and defeat the spirit of the world.

We don't need to be afraid of satan. We refuse to give him any honor. We won't even capitalize his name. He is nothing more than a fallen angel and is outnumbered 2 to 1 by Michael's and Gabriel's angelic forces. He is not all-knowing. He is not all-powerful. He is not everywhere-present. God is!

Jesus Christ defeated satan for you:

1. In the wilderness. Matt. 4 and Luke 4
2. In His sinless life. John 14:30, II Cor. 5:21
3. In His deliverance ministry. Matt. 12:22, 28-29
4. In His giving authority over all the power of the devil to us. Luke 10:17-19
5. In His fivefold, redemptive (buying us back from satan) act. His death, burial, bodily resurrection, ascension to heaven, and glorification. Col. 2:13-15; Eph. 1:20-21; Rom. 8:31-34
6. In His present intercessory prayer ministry on our behalf. Rom.8:34; I John 2:1-2

YOU RESIST SATAN THE SAME WAY THE LORD JESUS DID

1. By verbal confrontation based on the truth of God's Word. Matt. 4:1-11 with Luke 4:1-13
2. By refusing to act on his suggestions, even to the point of death. Rev. 12:11

SO HOW DO WE RID OURSELVES OF HIS INFLUENCE?

Jesus said, "I tell you the truth, whatever you bind on earth will be bound in heaven, and whatever you loose on earth will be loosed in heaven. (Matt. 16:19)" He has given us authority!

Luke 10:18-19 And he said to them, "I saw satan fall like lightning from heaven. Behold, I have given you authority to tread on serpents and scorpions, and over all the power of the enemy, and nothing shall hurt you. **Notice He gave us authority--not power. God has the power; satan has to submit to the authority of the name of Jesus Christ.** It is a seal, a permit, a writ of free passage we carry to pass through hostile territory. The enemy *has already been defeated and he knows it. BUT HE ONLY SUBMITS TO THOSE WHO PULL RANK ON HIM*! We have to use the authority given us."

It is like a true story we heard that happened during World War II. The Japanese had taken many American prisoners in the Philippines after General MacArthur left. They were held in prison camps. After America dropped the atom bombs on Hiroshima and Nagasaki, the Japanese surrendered. However, the American prisoners in the Philippines didn't know the enemy had surrendered because their Japanese captors didn't tell them. One day, an airplane with American markings landed on the airstrip outside the prison camp and an officer got out and walked to the edge of the barbed wire. He called out, "General! General! Come to the fence please!" When the emaciated, weak General drug his 95 pound frame to the fence the officer informed him that the Japanese had surrendered. With that information in hand, the General wheeled around and wobbled up to the office of the commanding officer of the camp and said, "My Commander in Chief has defeated your Commander in Chief! By the authority vested in me as one of his officers, I relieve you of command!" And he did. The prisoners were set free that day.

This ministry of Jesus Christ applies directly to you! You don't need to be in bondage to your addiction any more. Jesus has come to drive these influences from your life. You don't have to be powerful--just obedient. Jesus, your Commander in Chief, has defeated satan already.

Luke 11:17-26 "But he, knowing their thoughts, said to them, 'Every kingdom divided against itself is laid waste, and a divided household falls. And if satan also is divided against himself, how will his kingdom stand? For you say that I cast out demons by Beelzebul. And if I cast out demons by Beelzebul, by whom do your sons cast them out? Therefore they will be your judges. But if it is by the finger of God that I cast out demons, then the kingdom of God has come upon you. When a strong man, fully armed, guards his own palace, his goods are safe; but when one stronger than he attacks him and overcomes him, he takes away his armor in which he trusted and divides his spoil. Whoever is not with me is against me, and whoever does not gather with me scatters.' When the unclean spirit has gone out of a person, it passes through waterless places seeking rest, and finding none it says, 'I will return to my house from which I came.' And when it comes, it finds the house swept and put in order. Then it goes and brings seven other spirits more evil than itself, and they enter and dwell there. And the last state of that person is worse than the first." (ESV)

Now, taking all of this into account, let's look at what we are to do:

1. Put on the armor of God. Eph. 6:10-20
2. Bind the strongman.
3. Curse him and destroy his fruit
4. Kick him out.
5. Repair the damage done by him.
6. Fill the vacancy with the power of God and His Spirit.

So it is up to us to stop him, and God has given us all the tools we need.

Everything that bothers us is not the devil, but before we can effectively get on with dealing with our flesh, we must get rid of this culprit. Today, you will clean your house of the strongmen in your life. After they leave, you will become free to be the person God intended you to be and great changes can take place in your personality. You will feel clean and free.

Pray this prayer out loud:

Dear Heavenly Father, I come to you in Jesus' name, recognizing you as my Lord, Savior, Healer and Deliverer. You know all my problems, all the things that bind, torment, defile and harass me. Today I refuse to accept anything more from satan, and I loose myself from every dark spirit, from every evil influence, from every satanic bondage, and from every spirit, that is not the Spirit of God. I bind all these spirits up according to Matthew 18:18 where it says that whatever I bind on earth is bound in heaven, and whatever I loose on earth is loosed in heaven.

I ask you Father, to forgive me for allowing these spirits to manifest in my life, I purpose in my heart to serve you from now on.

satan, I rebuke you and all your evil spirits. I renounce any occult activities I've been involved in and renounce these strongmen and curse their fruit in me as Jesus did the fig tree. Right now I bind up and command these strongmen and their fruit to go directly to dark, dry places and stay there in Jesus' Name. Jesus has given me authority to use His Name, which is above all names.

I command the:

spirit of divination
familiar spirit
spirit of jealousy, anger, unforgiveness
lying spirit, guilt, self-condemnation
perverse and unclean spirits-pornography and lust, homosexuality, fornication and adultery
spirit of haughtiness, pride
spirit of heaviness, depression
spirit of whoredom--gluttony
spirit of infirmity, sickness and disease
dumb and deaf spirit
spirit of bondage (drugs and alcohol; cigarettes)
spirit of witchcraft and rebellion
spirit of lethargy
controlling spirit, judgmental and critical spirits
spirit of fear, anxiety, tormenting, driving spirits
seducing spirits
spirit of antichrist
spirit of error
spirit of confusion
spirit of death (self-destruction) and all their fruit to GO."

Take a deep breath and say, "GO…GO…GO!" These spirits have to leave.

We name all the spirits mentioned in Scripture to cover all the bases. Some of them may not have been involved in your life, but those who were are now gone. PRAISE GOD!!!

It is up to you to apply what you have learned and will learn, to walk free and to stay free. Don't let the evil one con you into reinfection.

We are now going to ask God to fill you with His Spirit. You are a new creation in Christ now. Speak to your Heavenly Father with confidence:

In Jesus' Name, I now call the Spirit of God to come and fill me to overflowing with God and His love. I loose upon myself the Holy Spirit and all His gifts:

> *The love of God*
> *The spirit of truth to set me free*
> *Power*
> *Love*
> *Sound mind*
> *Good and excellent spirit*
> *The spirit of purity*
> *A humble and contrite spirit*
> *The spirit of holiness*
> *The joy of the Lord*
> *The garment of praise*
> *The oil of gladness*
> *The comforter*
> *The gifts of healing and miracles, for by His stripes I am healed*
> *The spirit of adoption*
> *God's wisdom, knowledge and understanding*
> *The spirit of life, for no weapon formed against me will prosper*

What I have loosed on earth is loosed in heaven, and I call my body into chemical balance. Thank you Lord. I take authority over withdrawals. I speak to my thyroid, liver, kidneys, pancreas, pituitary, adrenal cortex and command them to function properly. I speak wholeness to my metabolism and my hormone balance. I command my immune system to function properly and my white cells to rise up and defeat sickness in my body.

In the Name of Jesus I command the pituitary gland to restructure the signals to my body, and for all the organs and glands and tissues to respond and be restored to the perfect order of God. I thank You, Father, for your special touch now upon me this very moment. In Jesus' Name.

Thank you Father for setting me free. I confess that my body is the temple for the Holy Spirit: I am redeemed, cleansed, sanctified, justified, healed and delivered by the blood of Jesus. Therefore, satan, from this day forward you have no place in me and no power over me, through the blood of Jesus.

Now, rejoice: it is done. You may feel lightheaded or feel a sense of great relief. However, some say they do not feel any different, or that they feel like going out and having another drink. If this is you, don't give up! You need more ministry. Contact the leader of this group and have them minister to you. Most of the time, these prayers are more effective when you have someone pray with you. But if you feel like nothing has happened, go through this checklist with your group leader:

1. This ministry may or may not involve your emotions. Things of the spirit are accomplished by faith--not emotions. You may not feel anything, but the next time you are tempted you will notice you are not susceptible. Something has happened. James 4:7 says that if you submit to God and tell the devil to flee, he has to go, no matter how you feel.

2. You need to be honest with yourself about how badly you want to be free. Did you really come into this time prepared to serve Jesus with all of your heart? Or were you looking for just another quick fix? James 1:2-8 talks about "double-mindedness" in the context of asking for wisdom but it applies here as well. Double-

mindedness is having one foot in the kingdom of God and the other in the kingdom of satan. God will not honor those types of prayers. Either you are committed to God or satan. There is no halfway as James relates, "But let him ask in faith, with no doubting, for the one who doubts is like a wave of the sea that is driven and tossed by the wind. For that person must not suppose that he will receive anything from the Lord; he is a double-minded man, unstable in all his ways".

3. Sometimes, it takes perseverance. James 1:2-8 again tells us, Count it all joy, my brothers, when you meet trials of various kinds, for you know that the testing of your faith produces steadfastness. And let steadfastness have its full effect, that you may be perfect and complete, lacking in nothing. Don't be bashful about asking to be prayed for again.

4. Evaluate whether or not there are still some things of the heart that were not released earlier. The Parable of the Sower tells us that satan can come and steal the Word from our heart if our heart is hard. Sometimes, there is a reluctance to truly release people from our judgment to God's judgment--we secretly hold on to them. If that is true, there is an area of our heart that is hard and the devil is able to steal what God has done.

5. Sometimes, that hardness of the heart is a defense mechanism that is there because of trauma early in our life. Many times, people are not aware of it because they have blocked it out of their memory. **This is especially true of sexual abuse**. If you have blank areas in your memory, talk to your group leader about where to go from here.

Step 5: Breaking Generation Curses

As we have already mentioned, these are things passed down from generation to generation through your family line. We take no chances. We pray against anything that might be there. You don't know if your ancestors were involved in occult practices. There are other things you know about such as "Irish temper," alcoholism, violence and so on.

Pray this prayer out loud:

In the Name of Jesus Christ, I now renounce, break and loose myself from all generation curses, psychic heredity, demonic holds, psychic powers, bondages--addictions to drugs or alcohol—bonds of physical or mental illness, or curses upon me or my family line as a result of sins, transgression, iniquities, occult or psychic involvement of myself, my parents, or any of my ancestors. I break the power of all evil words spoken out against me from the day I was conceived in my mother's womb until this moment, in Jesus' Name. Thank you, Lord Jesus, for setting me free!!

Step 6: Breaking Soul Ties:

Soul ties are not called by that name in the Bible, but the ripple effect of their devastation is clear throughout Scripture. These are the ties we have with everyone we have had sexual relations with outside of marriage. God is not embarrassed about sex. He invented it! But sex was reserved for the marriage bed. It is reserved for the marriage bed **because in marriage, a man and woman become *one* in flesh, soul and spirit**. Until just recent times, it was sexual intercourse that confirmed a marriage. That is why we used to have "shot gun" weddings. That is why Jesus said He would allow divorce in case of adultery because the unfaithful mate had become one in flesh and spirit with someone else and thereby, broke the marriage covenant.

Addictions to sex and drugs often go hand in hand. Soul ties help explain the phenomenon. Soul ties also explain why you may not be satisfied with your mate—there are still ties with these people in your past. Those ties need to be broken. Please read the following scriptures:

Mal 2:13-15 "And this second thing you do. You cover the LORD's altar with tears, with weeping and groaning because he no longer regards the offering or accepts it with favor from your hand. But you say, 'Why does he not?' Because the LORD was witness between you and the wife of your youth, to whom you have been faithless, though she is your companion and your wife by covenant. Did he not make them one, with a portion of the Spirit in their union? And what was the one God seeking? Godly offspring. So guard yourselves in your spirit, and let none of you be faithless to the wife of your youth."

I Cor 6:16-20 "Or do you not know that he who is joined to a prostitute becomes one body with her? For, as it is written, 'The two will become one flesh.' But he who is joined to the Lord becomes one spirit with him. Flee from sexual immorality. Every other sin a person commits is outside the body, but the sexually immoral person sins against his own body. Or do you not know that your body is a temple of the Holy Spirit within you, whom you have from God? You are not your own, for you were bought with a price. So glorify God in your body."

Pray this prayer out loud:

Father, in the Name of Jesus, I submit my soul, my desires and my emotions to your Spirit. I confess as sin, all my promiscuous, premarital sexual relationships and all sexual relationships outside of marriage. I confess all my ungodly spirit, soul, and body ties as sin. I thank You for forgiving me and cleansing me right now!

Father, thank you for giving me the keys of Your kingdom, the keys of spiritual authority. What I bind is bound and what I loose is loosed. In Jesus' name, I ask You to cut and loose me from all soulish ties to past sexual partners and ungodly relationships. Please uproot all the tentacles of sexual bondage, of emotional longings and dependencies, and of enslaving thoughts. I bind, renounce, and resist any evil spirits that have reinforced those soul ties or may have been transferred to me or my mate and have defiled us through evil associations.

Please cleanse my soul and help me to forget all illicit unions so that I am free to give my soul totally to you and to my mate or future mate. Father, I receive Your forgiveness for all past sexual sins. Thank You for remembering my sins no more. Thank You for cleansing me from all unrighteousness. I commit myself totally to You. By Your grace, please keep me holy in my spirit, soul, and body. I praise You and thank You. In Jesus' Name, Amen!!

If you're married, ask God to heal the marriage relationship.
A word of caution: It is not wise to tell your mate of previous premarital sexual encounters or adulterous affairs. You must really have the direction of the Lord and the timing must be right if you are going to tell. I (Theo) have seen marriages devastated by people believing their mate must know *everything* about them. The demand to know everything about you from your mate can often be a symptom of his or her own insecurities about you and when you confess your past, your mate suddenly becomes convinced you can no longer be trusted.

Step 7. Rebellion Against God:

Many people have had a rebellious attitude towards God since childhood and have never recognized it as such. They are in situations, families, or jobs **that God did not cause but are consciously or unconsciously blaming Him**. They are suffering the second temptation of Christ in the wilderness (Matt. 4:1-11). satan is able to accuse God before them. They often don't come out and say that is what is going on, but it comes out in other subtle ways.

Consider this question: say that prior to birth, God came by asking for volunteers to come to earth and live. Would you:

1. Volunteer?
2. If so, would you choose this century or another one?
3. If you had a choice, would you:
        Choose the same parents? (If they weren't abusive)
            Mother?
            Father?
4. Would you be a boy or a girl?
5. Choose the same body?

6. Choose your same face?
7. Choose your mind, character, personality?
8. If you are a woman, are you:

       Pretty?

       Attractive?

       Desirable?

       Beautiful?

       Lovable?

9. If you are a man, are you:

       Handsome?

       Attractive?

       Good-looking?

       Desirable?

10. If God came to you today and gave you a choice, "You can either go with me to heaven right now or go all the way through life," which would you choose?

If you said "No" to many of these questions, there is a good chance that you hold some anger towards God.

We have learned that we must extend grace to ourselves before we can really love ourselves. The Great Commandment commands us to love our neighbor AS ourselves. We are to love ourselves.

We are not saying that you are to be content with your negative traits, otherwise there would be no reason for this class and this manual! *We are saying to be content with those things you cannot change.* Sound familiar? You are not God and there are some things you can't change. We must be reconciled to God and learn to love **being us**, or it will affect us in many ways. It directly affects our relationship with the Father, our ability and confidence to help others--even the ability to sustain our health.

Pray this prayer out loud:

Dear Heavenly Father, in Jesus' Name I've come to You to confess I have not been too happy with what You have created me to be. I have been disgusted and disgruntled at my situation--some of it directed at my parents. I've looked at others and coveted their looks and family situations. I have been upset.

I have not even realized I have been committing sin and rebellion against You! I did not understand that when you put me in my family, You intended to bring glory out of those conditions. I have not properly trusted you and I confess that today.

I admit I have been in spiritual rebellion. I've resisted my own body. I have not been able to love my brothers and sisters, mate and family as I want to. Lord, I want to be reconciled to my proper time and place, so forgive me for my ignorance.

Your Word says that people perish for lack of knowledge, and I recognize that some of this is flesh and some of it is caused by allowing a spirit of rebellion. Father, forgive me for hurting You.

Now, satan, in Jesus' Name, I bind up the spirit of rebellion, according to Matthew 18:18, cast it out, and call in a humble and contrite spirit and the of Spirit of God!

And now, dear Father, I want to be closer to You and to being myself. Teach me to love what You are building me into, so I can love being myself and learn to reach out and love others, not in conceit or pride but in gratitude that I am made in Your image.

I thank You, Father, that You are reaching back right now into my past and healing those wounds I have suffered since birth. You whisper to me, "I did not make anyone else like you--nobody else has a voice like yours; even your finger prints are unique. Just as no two snowflakes are the same, I made you to be my unique glory, and I love you just as you are." Thank You, Jesus. Amen.

We want to stop now and make sure you understand something. Now that you have renounced the enemy and cleaned your house, it doesn't mean he is going to give up. We don't want to leave the impression that the devil and his demons are behind every bush and ready to jump out and get you. But, on the other hand, it is a certainty that as a Christian you can count on a battle.

From now on, you *must* learn to separate the battle you will be in with the enemy from what is your own responsibility. You can't blame everything on the devil--that's what Eve did. On the other hand, you can't ignore the battle. **Jesus told us to pray in the Lord's Prayer,"…And lead us not into temptation, but deliver us from the evil one."** (Matt.6:13) The disciples asked Him to teach them to pray because they noticed He went off and prayed and then was able to do miracles. It was something He did every day. In this last part of the prayer, He draws attention to:

1. You will be in a battle with the evil one.

2. There will be a personal responsibility to resist temptation because it is the devil's territory. If you don't stop and realize what is going on, God will allow you to be tempted so that you see that there still is a strong hold in your life. If you ignore your personal responsibility and the battle at hand, it is likely you will fall back into your old patterns.

3. There is a supernatural element to the battle-i.e., the evil one is defeated by God.

Every Christian's life should include intercession and warfare, *whether or not they have been addicted.* Therefore, from now on pray these prayers *aloud every day.*

Armor of God: Ephesians 6:10-20

I am strong in You Lord, and in the power of Your might. I put on the whole armor of God and do stand against the plans of the devil. In the Name of Jesus, I bind satan and the principalities, the powers, the rulers of the darkness of this world. I bind and cast down spiritual wickedness in high places and render them harmless and ineffective against me and my loved ones. I resist you, devil, in the name of Jesus, and I stand my ground.
I have the belt of truth buckled around my waist--the truth of God that sets me free! I have on the breastplate of righteousness that covers my body, my heart and vital organs and show me I am in right standing with my God! My feet are shod with the preparation of the gospel of peace, and I take those feet and tread on serpents and scorpions, for I have been given authority over all of your power. I take the helmet of salvation and cover my head securely, for I have the mind of Christ. The only spirit I will follow is the Spirit of the living God that lives inside me and speaks to me from within.
I take the shield of faith and quench every arrow you throw at me, devil! I take the sword of the Spirit, which is the Word of God, and pierce through your wicked plans, for it is written all I have to do is submit myself to God, and tell you to flee, and you have to go…so GO!! In the Name of Jesus.
I place the blood of Jesus over me, my family, my home, my ministry, my place of employment, my bank account, my debts, my car and possessions--all of which belong to God--and I serve notice that your power is broken, devil, over me and mine, in Jesus' Name.
Thank you Father. Send people my way to minister to today. Amen

A Prayer of Protection:

Father, because I dwell in the secret place of the Most High, I pray that I will remain stable and fixed under the shadow of You, almighty God, whose power no one can withstand. I say of You Lord, "You are my refuge and my fortress, my God, on whom I rely and confidently trust." For You deliver me from the snare of the fowler, deadly pestilence, terrors of night, evil plots of the wicked and destruction or sudden death. Thank You that You will never leave me nor forsake me, but as I call upon You, you will be with me even in times of trouble to deliver me, satisfying me with long life! All of this is true because I have set my love on You, and I know Your Name. Be it done unto me and my family according to Your Word.
Amen.

STEP 4. HEALING THE ADDICTIVE MIND SET

God is very clear about the power of our minds. You are headed, right at this instant, towards your most dominant thought! If your thoughts are positive, you will find yourself acting out positively. But if they are negative, you will find yourself back in your old patterns. *If you take care of the addictive root and do not take care of the addictive mindset, you eventually will go back into your addiction.* You can be set free from a spirit of fear but if you still hold on to deep seated beliefs of doom and destruction around every corner, you will not be free.

This is the step that those who relapse fail to follow through on. Invariably, as we talk to these individuals, we find that they have not attempted this step, or have started and given up. Remember, we told you at the front of this manual that you would have to change how you think, live, relate to people and a number of other things. There is nothing passive about this step. There is nothing quick about this step--it will take your effort and patience.

The mind is the most powerful organ you have in your body. *Your body will simply do what your mind tells it to do.* Your emotions and *physiology do not know the difference between truth and falsehood.* Therefore, much of the inner turmoil you have experienced is caused by your perception of life. These perceptions were formed while you were growing and maturing. THE QUESTION IS, ARE THEY TRUE? Examine this diagram closely:

It is not safe to say the mind is like a computer. It is much more complicated and sophisticated than that. The number of possible connections between neurons in your brain is 10^{800}. That is more than the total number of *atoms* in the universe! It may be a highly sophisticated information gatherer and sorter, but it has an observer who runs it--"You".

Any human has strong patterns of learned perceptions concerning life. These patterns are ingrained early in life as we have already learned. For addicts, these patterns have become more deeply ingrained than in other people-- so much so that they don't see life realistically.

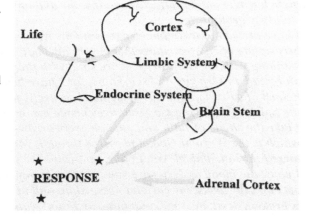

Cortex: This is the part of your brain that evaluates what you are seeing and hearing. It decides whether you are being *attacked or threatened.* **But, its evaluation is based on past imprints!** Therefore, in the addictive mindset, your mind formed conclusions about life that were necessary to survive during a time in your life. The problem is, that those warped conclusions are not valid now, and do not work in real life.

Limbic System: This is the part of your brain that feels emotion. **It feels emotion as the cortex feeds it information.** If the cortex evaluates and decides you are being attacked or threatened, you feel anger or fear. The point is, YOUR THOUGHTS *CAUSE* YOUR EMOTIONS! This is *very* important for you to understand, because many people feel out of control because they believe they can't control their emotions and therefore might go back to drugs. This is not the case.

Brain Stem: This is the part of the Central Nervous System that houses the automatic physiologic responses of your body. Once the Limbic System has been told to feel anger or fear, it signals the endocrine system (hormones) and the brain stem, telling it to signal other parts of the body to speed up respiration, heart rate and blood pressure. This is why you start to quiver and shake when you are very angry but don't express it. Your body is telling you to FIGHT OR RUN, but you can't because it is inappropriate. You are like a rocket on the launching pad that has been fired but remains tied down. There is a tremendous amount of energy that is internalized, but going nowhere! If this continues, it will destroy you physically, and you will turn back to chemicals to anesthetize the pain. THIS HAS ALL BEEN CAUSED BY A MIND THAT HAS BEEN

PROGRAMMED TO INTERPRET WHAT IT SEES INCORRECTLY. It overreacts, overprotects, over just about everything to protect its master. It has been programmed to believe it should be like God, and panics because it cannot follow through with its original command. It behaves like a computer infected with a "computer virus" introduced by a villain.

It is interesting that your "YOU" has been reacting emotionally for years to the data this marvelous organ has been giving it without even questioning if it is true or false. Most of your anger and/or fear has been unnecessary simply because your "computer" has been programmed incorrectly.

The good news is that you can change that! This is one area where you have total control *if you know what to do*. If a warped perception of life can bring panic, it is just as true that a realistic view of life can bring peace. That is what we are about to set out to do.

John 8:31-32 "So Jesus said to the Jews who had believed him, 'If you abide in my word, you are truly my disciples, and you will know the truth, and the truth will set you free.'"

As you review the Genesis Factor spiral again, remember how satan led Adam and Eve astray by taking the truth and twisting it just enough to make it sound possible. In fact, if you read closely what God actually said to Adam and compare it with what satan says, his twisting of the truth is so clever it may not be apparent to you at first. This has happened to you.

IT ISN'T SO MUCH WHAT HAPPENED TO YOU IN LIFE THAT CAUSED THE PROBLEMS; THE PROBLEMS WERE CAUSED BY YOUR FAULTY OR UNTRUE *CONCLUSIONS* ABOUT THOSE EVENTS.

Changing your addictive mindset consists of two definite, but different, components:

    1. The first is flushing out the misbelief you have picked up over the years.

    2. The other is saturating your mind with the truth. This is meditation.

Please read the following scriptures and answer the questions:

Eph 4:22-24 "That, in reference to your former manner of life, you lay aside the old self, which is being corrupted in accordance with the lusts of deceit, and that you be renewed in the spirit of your mind, and put on the new self, which in the likeness of God has been created in righteousness and holiness of the truth." (ESV)

What do you think your responsibility is to "be renewed in the spirit of your mind"?

Who is going to "lay aside", "be renewed..." and "put on…" in this scripture--you or God?

Rom 8:5-6 "For those who live according to the flesh set their minds on the things of the flesh, but those who live according to the Spirit set their minds on the things of the Spirit. For to set the mind on the flesh is death, but to set the mind on the Spirit is life and peace." (ESV)

What does this scripture say is *the* controlling factor determining whether you follow after the Spirit or your old ways?

Rom 12:2 "Do not be conformed to this world, but be transformed by the renewal of your mind, that by testing you may discern what is the will of God, what is good and acceptable and perfect."

The word "transformed" comes from a Greek word that means "metamorphosis" (cocoon to butterfly). Based on that fact is being changed by the renewing of your mind a process or a quick fix?

Does it take your effort?

I hope by now that you are not still hung up on whether the Bible says it is OK to heal the mind. OF COURSE IT DOES! Yet, there are still well-meaning Christians who say, "Well, that's psychology and that is of the world--not God!" They don't know their Bible.

Let's get on with your healing process.

Changing your addictive mindset will entail reprogramming the source of your information. This will be in three areas:

> **Self-statements**
> **Evaluation**
> **Expectations**

SELF STATEMENTS

Realize that you have "inner murmuring" going on constantly. We call this self-talk. It has been there all along. If it is negative, you will be negative. If it is positive, you will be positive.

This is one area where you can start to see IMMEDIATE reduction in your negative emotion level. Essentially, the process starts with telling yourself the truth and learning to challenge the lies. How many times have you thought something like, "If so and so does that one more time...!" Those are the kinds of thoughts that fire you up.

Here is an example of a common sequence that will cause an outburst:

"Boy, I'm sure tired. They work my tail off on this job! I wish I could get out of here and get something better. Not likely! It would help a little bit if they would acknowledge my effort--but they don't. Boy, it's hot! I wonder if that Pepsi is still in the refrigerator at home. I'm going to gulp it down as soon as I get home--if it's still there. It probably won't be. No one thinks about anyone but himself around that family. Those kids had two cans of pop a piece last night. I've got to watch them like a hawk or they'll eat everything. They don't appreciate how much money things cost. They don't appreciate how hard I work for that pop! As a matter of fact, they don't appreciate me! My wife should make them aware of how hard I work for them."

What do you think will happen when he gets home?

You may have laughed at those thoughts and you may laugh at what you see on paper from your own thoughts.

This is an example of some actual self-talk by a man who was deeply depressed and suicidal. He was asked to write down the actual thoughts in his mind *ONLY WHEN HE FELT NEGATIVE EMOTIONS*. Below the self-statements, I have written the lies I see in his thoughts.

October 11 depressed; angry	It doesn't matter what I do, I'll fail. Everyone does better at this job than I do. I always pick the wrong choices. If I fail one more time, I don't know if I can take it. It isn't fair!! God, you bless everyone else. Why not me!! What's the use? The more I pray the worse it gets. No one understands.

October 13 anger	Why doesn't she listen to me? She never listens to me!!
	No matter what I do, she'll never be pleased
	Not only that, she has turned the kids against me.
	She talks bad about me behind my back.
	If people would only do what I tell them, everything would be OK.

October 14 depression; anxiety	My God! What's going to happen to me!!? What am I doing wrong?
	If God doesn't undertake, I'm going to go down. Doesn't he care?
	If I don't gross $800 this week, it's all over.
	I must really be a dud.

1. Lie= My worth equals my performance (since my performance is poor, I'm no good and will continue to be so).

   Truth= My worth is in "being" (I'm a child of the King)--not "having."

2. Lie= To fail is unbearable; disastrous.

   Truth= I will survive if it doesn't turn out. God is with me.

3. Lie= God shows His approval by blessing with money.

   Truth= No, He doesn't! I'm already approved through Jesus. He bought me for a mighty price and He doesn't buy junk.

4. Lie= For me to be happy, people must do right and things have to go right.

   Truth= It is normal for people and events to be imperfect.

This man was deeply religious. One of the above lies was the key to unlocking his freedom. Which one do you think it was and why?

Do you see his addictive mindset?

PROJECT:

Let's start looking at your negative thoughts as **pests**. They peck and buzz and irritate you until you blow up. However, you've not trapped them. You've not really looked at them. For the next **four weeks** *every* time you feel anger, stop and record what is *ACTUALLY* in your thoughts. You will have to be brutally honest with yourself because your tendency will be to reject them or not want your group or pastor to see them. TRAP THEM!! There are usually only 5-8 statements for every episode. By the end of four weeks you should have at least 12 pages of writing. If you don't, you are not trying to get in touch with your feelings. Don't be afraid of them; they can't harm you.

DATE	EMOTION	ACTUAL THOUGHTS

DATE	EMOTION	ACTUAL THOUGHTS

Do you notice any patterns?

Here are some well-known addictive belief systems.[13] See if you can identify with any of them, using your self-talk notes. **Place numbers from the following list alongside any of your self-talk statements that fit.**

1. I should be perfect.
2. I should be all powerful. That is, I should be able to control every part of my environment.
3. I should always get what I want.
4. I should always get what I want without pain.
5. I am powerless. I can't do anything about my situation.
6. Feelings are dangerous.
7. External "things" will give me the power I need--i.e., belongings, money, and friends.
8. Image is everything. I have to look good.
9. I should be able to meet my needs *indirectly*. For instance, if I really need love, I will believe I should wait for it and pour my energy into "things" I love in the meantime.

Look for patterns like:

Hyperbole-	This is overstating the case. Words like "always, never, every time." They are black and white, all or nothing words. Using them causes you to be rigid and not see other options.
Performance-	These are statements that connect your ability to perform with your worth as a human being.
Catastrophizing-	This is insisting that the worst possible thing is going to happen if….
Paranoia-	This is reading an attack or threat into people's actions or expressions without asking them what was *really intended*.
Victim-	This has to do with statements that imply your life is out of your control and outside forces are working against you.

These are some of the common patterns. Go over these statements with your pastor or your group. What are some of the obvious half-truths about your statements?

Romans 12:1-2 Read this carefully. Notice the essential elements of this passage in gaining victory in your life.

1. Give yourself totally to God. Your attitude is everything now. Pray with an attitude of repentance (changing your mind; being willing to change your mind).

2. Stop conforming to old patterns. Breaking these patterns will take your ACTIVE involvement. The command here is "to be transformed by the renewing of your mind." It doesn't happen by osmosis. It takes challenging these old ways of thinking. If you allow your mind to remain passive, old patterns will win out.

3. Replace the lies with the truth. This is the renewing.

PROJECT: FOR THE NEXT THREE TO FOUR MONTHS

1. STOP! Every time you are *feeling* negative emotion, train yourself to stop and identify the emotion. You are to be like a sentry and stop all possible threats to your mind and identify them before allowing them to proceed.

2. IDENTIFY THE NEGATIVE SELF-TALK. Allow it to go through to completion BRIEFLY. Don't dwell on it.

3. IDENTIFY THE CORRESPONDING MISBELIEF. This self-statement will fit into one of the categories you have discovered. An example would be like one of those on page 51 that give an example of self-talk.

4. REPLACE THAT THOUGHT BY QUOTING ALOUD THE CORRESPONDING TRUTH. Say it over several times.

5. ACT ON THE TRUTH, IMMEDIATELY, IF AT ALL POSSIBLE. This is to reinforce the truth. Doing something physical to reinforce the truth will cause these thoughts to take hold. In the past, you have acted on the negative thoughts and become bound.

Meditation:

New Age or Far Eastern meditations are not Biblical. They ask you to *empty* your mind. That is dangerous. They are passive.

Biblical meditation *is not passive, but ACTIVE*. It concentrates on the Word of God.

The word for meditation in the Bible is "hagah" which means "to murmur". It has another root word "higgayown", which carries the meaning "to chew upon". It is a picture word of a cow chewing its cud. It's an active word that has to do with murmuring or rehashing the Word of God in your mind.

The question immediately arises, "How can you hold to Christ's teachings if His teachings are not in your mind?" It is very difficult. As a troubled Christian, the old tapes seem to drown out the Holy Spirit in our lives.

The Word of God is powerful **if** it is hidden in our hearts. It is the "owner's manual" for how we were made to live. If we live in another way, we don't do well.

All of the following scriptures have to do with biblical meditation. Read them carefully and apply them. If you do, your life will change dramatically.

Joshua 1:8   In your own words, what are the specific promises you see here for your life?

Psalms 1:1-3   Besides meditating on the truth, what does this say to you about adopting thought patterns that come from negative people?

Psalms 19:14   How do you see that this prayer of David's challenges the negative self-talk we covered in the last section?

Psalms 119   Read this chapter in its entirety. Circle every time it refers to meditation and underline the promises that go with it.

Phil. 4:4-13   Notice that Paul is letting us in on a profound secret of his! How to be content. Part of his secret has to do with mediating on good things. It isn't the whole package, but an important part. How do you see that the rest of his secret falls in line with what you have learned in this booklet so far?

II Pet. 1:1-11   Both Peter and Paul were angry men at one time. Peter gives us a secret of his in this passage. He was a man who was both angry and impulsive--a bad combination. Look closely at the steps he lays out to gain *self-control.*

1. He says we already have faith, that it was a gift from God.
2. Therefore, we already have power to live a full and godly life free from hostility.
3. That God has given us *great and precious promises* so that through them *we might participate in the divine nature*…Where are the promises? In the Bible.
4. We have to ACT on the above truths. He says we need to make every effort to:

   a. Set our minds to do good. This is foundational. You cannot have self-control unless you first set your mind to do good.

   b. Knowledge. This is not the same word that is used for knowing God. *It is the knowledge of the **promises of God** mentioned in verse 4*! **This is the Key.**

   c. **Now** you can develop self-control--not before.

Romans 8:5-7   Paul says you will continue to follow after your addictive nature if you have your mind set on what that nature desires.

                How does meditation on God's Word help a person follow after the Spirit?

                Look at verse 13. According to this verse, how are you going to bury those old angry patterns?

How can you follow after the Holy Spirit, if the words of the Spirit are not in your mind?

What kind of dangers do you see if a person tries to rely only on "his inner voice" without taking the Word of God into his mind?

Before the Word of God can be chewed on, it must be swallowed and digested. This comes down to a very simple truth. **You must read it and memorize it!** But that's works! No, it isn't. It's a prescription for wholeness. Peter says, "make every effort."

Well, who can memorize the whole Bible?

No one can, but Peter didn't refer to the whole Bible, he referred to the **promises.**

PROJECT: If you have a Bible that is hard to read, get one that is not. I recommend the New International Version. It is in plain English. Your Bible should have study helps in it. I recommend the Thompson Chain-Reference Bible in the NIV. This has a small concordance, a word study section, and so on.

After you get such a Bible, look up all the promises regarding what you are working through. For instance, if it's anger, look up all the promises having to do with peace. If it's fear, then look up all the promises that have to do with protection, ect…

Memorize the scriptures that really stick out to you and murmur them throughout the day. Make this a lifestyle from now on. **Here are some scriptures to get you started. We have listed some scriptures that have to do with three of the fruits of the Holy Spirit—Love, joy and peace.**

Project:

1. *Each morning*, **pick one scripture each from love, joy and peace; write them down on note cards. Commit them to memory and murmur them to yourself throughout the day. The next day, pick three new ones.**

2. Using your new Bible, *start your own list* **of promises for the rest of the fruit of the Holy Spirit. You will find a list of the fruits in Galatians 5:22**

You will be amazed how much your emotions begin to be healed as you "have your mind set on what the Holy Spirit desires". You will be experiencing "being made new in the attitude of your mind".

LOVE

Ps 13:5 **But I have trusted in your steadfast love; my heart shall rejoice in your salvation**

Ps 23:1-6 The LORD is my shepherd; I shall not want. He makes me lie down in green pastures. He leads me beside still waters. He restores my soul. He leads me in paths of righteousness for his name's sake. Even though I walk through the valley of the shadow of death, I will fear no evil, for you are with me; your rod and your staff, they comfort me. You prepare a table before me in the presence of my enemies; you anoint my head with oil; my cup overflows. Surely goodness and mercy shall follow me all the days of my life, and I shall dwell in the house of the LORD forever

Ps 25:7 Remember not the sins of my youth or my transgressions; according to your steadfast love remember me, for the sake of your goodness, O LORD!

Ps 31:7 I will rejoice and be glad in your steadfast love, because you have seen my affliction; you have known the distress of my soul,

Ps 32:10 Many are the sorrows of the wicked, but steadfast love surrounds the one who trusts in the LORD.

Ps 33:18 Behold, the eye of the LORD is on those who fear him, on those who hope in his steadfast love,

Ps 48:9 We have thought on your steadfast love, O God, in the midst of your temple.

Ps 59:16 But I will sing of your strength; I will sing aloud of your steadfast love in the morning. For you have been to me a fortress and a refuge in the day of my distress.

Ps 63:3 Because your steadfast love is better than life, my lips will praise you.

Ps 86:13 For great is your steadfast love toward me; you have delivered my soul from the depths of Sheol.

Ps 100:5 For the LORD is good; his steadfast love endures forever, and his faithfulness to all generations.

Ps 103:2-5 Bless the LORD, O my soul, and forget not all his benefits, who forgives all your iniquity, who heals all your diseases, who redeems your life from the pit,
who crowns you with steadfast love and mercy, who satisfies you with good so that your youth is renewed like the eagle's.

Ps 107:1 Oh give thanks to the LORD, for he is good, for his steadfast love endures forever!

Ps 107:43 Whoever is wise, let him attend to these things; let them consider the steadfast love of the LORD.

John 3:16 "For God so loved the world, that he gave his only Son, that whoever believes in him should not perish but have eternal life.

John 15:10 If you keep my commandments, you will abide in my love, just as I have kept my Father's commandments and abide in his love.

Romans 8:39 nor height nor depth, nor anything else in all creation, will be able to separate us from the love of God in Christ Jesus our Lord.

2 Cor 5:14 For the love of Christ controls us, because we have concluded this: that one has died for all, therefore all have died and he died for all, that those who live might no longer live for themselves but for him who for their sake died and was raised.

Eph 1:4-5 even as he chose us in him before the foundation of the world, that we should be holy and blameless before him. In love he predestined us for adoption as sons through Jesus Christ, according to the purpose of his will

Eph 2:3-5 among whom we all once lived in the passions of our flesh, carrying out the desires of the body and the mind, and were by nature children of wrath, like the rest of mankind. But God, being rich in mercy, because of the great love with which he loved us, even when we were dead in our trespasses, made us alive together with Christ—by grace you have been saved—

I John 4:9 In this the love of God was made manifest among us, that God sent his only Son into the world, so that we might live through him.

I John 4:19 We love because he first loved us.

JOY

Ps 16:11 You make known to me the path of life; in your presence there is fullness of joy; at your right hand are pleasures forevermore.

Ps 19:8 the precepts of the LORD are right, rejoicing the heart; the commandment of the LORD is pure, enlightening the eyes;

Ps 28:7 The LORD is my strength and my shield; in him my heart trusts, and I am helped; my heart exults, and with my song I give thanks to him.

Ps 30:11 You have turned for me my mourning into dancing; you have loosed my sackcloth and clothed me with gladness,

Ps 94:19 When the cares of my heart are many, your consolations cheer my soul.

Ps 126:5 Those who sow in tears shall reap with shouts of joy!

Ps 126:6 He who goes out weeping, bearing the seed for sowing, shall come home with shouts of joy, bringing his sheaves with him.

Prov 12:20 Deceit is in the heart of those who devise evil, but those who plan peace have joy.

Isaiah 61:7 Instead of your shame there shall be a double portion; instead of dishonor they shall rejoice in their lot; therefore in their land they shall possess a double portion; they shall have everlasting joy.

John 15:11 These things I have spoken to you, that my joy may be in you, and that your joy may be full.

John 16:22 So also you have sorrow now, but I will see you again, and your hearts will rejoice, and no one will take your joy from you.

John 16:24 Until now you have asked nothing in my name. Ask, and you will receive, that your joy may be full.

Acts 2:28 You have made known to me the paths of life; you will make me full of gladness with your presence.'

Romans 15:13 May the God of hope fill you with all joy and peace in believing, so that by the power of the Holy Spirit you may abound in hope.

Heb 12:2 looking to Jesus, the founder and perfecter of our faith, who for the joy that was set before him endured the cross, despising the shame, and is seated at the right hand of the throne of God.

I Pet 1:8 Though you have not seen him, you love him. Though you do not now see him, you believe in him and rejoice with joy that is inexpressible and filled with glory,

PEACE

Ps 4:8 In peace I will both lie down and sleep; for you alone, O LORD, make me dwell in safety.

Ps 29:11 May the LORD give strength to his people! May the LORD bless his people with peace!

Ps 37:11 But the meek shall inherit the land and delight themselves in abundant peace.

Ps 37:37 Mark the blameless and behold the upright, for there is a future for the man of peace.

Ps 85:8 Let me hear what God the LORD will speak, for he will speak peace to his people, to his saints; but let them not turn back to folly.

Ps 119:165 Great peace have those who love your law; nothing can make them stumble.

Prov 12:20 Deceit is in the heart of those who devise evil, but those who plan peace have joy.

Prov 14:30 A tranquil heart gives life to the flesh, but envy makes the bones rot.

Isaiah 26:3 You keep him in perfect peace whose mind is stayed on you, because he trusts in you.

Isaiah 32:17 And the effect of righteousness will be peace, and the result of righteousness, quietness and trust forever.

Isaiah 53:5 But he was pierced for our transgressions; he was crushed for our iniquities; upon him was the chastisement that brought us peace, and with his wounds we are healed.

Isaiah 54:10 For the mountains may depart and the hills be removed, but my steadfast love shall not depart from you, and my covenant of peace shall not be removed," says the LORD, who has compassion on you.

Isaiah 54:13 All your children shall be taught by the LORD, and great shall be the peace of your children.

Isaiah 55:12 "For you shall go out in joy and be led forth in peace; the mountains and the hills before you shall break forth into singing, and all the trees of the field shall clap their hands.

Isaiah 57:2 The latter glory of this house shall be greater than the former, says the LORD of hosts. And in this place I will give peace, declares the LORD of hosts.'"

Haggai 2:9 The latter glory of this house shall be greater than the former, says the LORD of hosts. And in this place I will give peace, declares the LORD of hosts.'"

Luke 2:14 "Glory to God in the highest, and on earth peace among those with whom he is pleased!"

John 14:27 Peace I leave with you; my peace I give to you. Not as the world gives do I give to you. Let not your hearts be troubled, neither let them be afraid

John 16:33 I have said these things to you, that in me you may have peace. In the world you will have tribulation. But take heart; I have overcome the world."

Eph 2:14,15 For he himself is our peace, who has made us both one and has broken down in his flesh the dividing wall of hostility by abolishing the law of commandments expressed in ordinances, that he might create in himself one new man in place of the two, so making peace,

Phil 4:7 And the peace of God, which surpasses all understanding, will guard your hearts and your minds in Christ Jesus.

Phil 4:9 What you have learned and received and heard and seen in me—practice these things, and the God of peace will be with you.

Heb 12:11 For the moment all discipline seems painful rather than pleasant, but later it yields the peaceful fruit of righteousness to those who have been trained by it

James 3:18 And a harvest of righteousness is sown in peace by those who make peace.

EVALUATION

This is the process by which you answer the question, "Am I being **R**ejected, **A**ttacked or **T**hreatened (**R.A.T**)? And if I am, is it worth getting upset over?"

Most of the time, your overreaction is unjustified. What you perceive as R.A.T. is not life or health threatening. In other words, anger other than a response to life or health jeopardizing threats or attack, IS NEUROTIC.

To change your addictive mind-set you must learn to challenge your old way of evaluating circumstances by asking yourself the: DOES THIS MAKE ANY ETERNAL DIFFERENCE?

For instance, if someone comes at you with a club and you are convinced it isn't time to go be with the Lord, you had better get angry fast! However, if you are hostile because someone did not accept your suggestion at a group meeting, BIG DEAL! It makes no eternal difference.

As Christians, we make much to-do about matters we think make a great deal of eternal difference. To qualify, they must pass this test:

WOULD JESUS SAY IT? WOULD JESUS DO IT?

There are some things Jesus got hostile about. Injustice and abuse were two of them. But beyond those, you don't see Him getting hostile.

If Jesus were in your shoes, what kinds of things would He get upset over?

What kinds of things would not upset Him, but do upset you?

PROJECT:

1. Evaluate the scenario of the man with the Pepsi. In detail, tear apart his "right to be angry." Really let him have it!

2. Go back and do the same thing for your Life History.

3. In how many things was your anger justified?

Evaluation also has to do with *putting yourself in the other person's shoes*. Go back to your **Self Talk Diary** on page 50, and write how you think the people who triggered your emotion may have felt during each episode.

1.
2.
3.
4.
5.
6.
7.
8.
9.
10.
11.
12.
13.
14.
15.
16.
17.
18.

Evaluation also means TAKING TIME. Counting to 10 is old, but it works. Counting to 10 gives you time to evaluate what is really going on.

TAKING A TIME-OUT is often necessary. If you feel you are going to blow up, tell the person you need a time-out to evaluate what is going on.

EACH TIME YOU FEEL STRONG EMOTIONS SUCH AS ANGER, STOP! EVALUATE WHETHER YOU HAVE THE RIGHT TO BE ANGRY.

Sometimes, you can make yourself angry simply by dwelling on something from your past. Even after you think you have forgiven those in your history, it is possible to pick up the anger against them again by going back, picking it up and chewing on it. The problem with meditating on negative things is that they become bigger than real life. Things get blown out of proportion in your mind. RESIST CHEWING IT OVER AGAIN. If you have released these things, don't pick them up again. All the rules of evaluation apply.

PROJECT: Enlist the help of someone who knows you well and spends a lot of time with you. When you daydream and he or she can tell you are going over something in your mind again, share what you are thinking and allow yourself to be challenged.

EXPECTATIONS

We all have reasonable expectations. If I flip the light switch, I expect the light to come on. If I pay my power bill, I expect to receive electricity. Unrealistic expectations, however, can produce anger. We often rely on certain responses or behaviors from people who are unable or unwilling to meet our want. If we continue to insist on their compliance, they become a threat to our view of rightness. They reject our perceived right to have our own way. We feel we have the right to expect more.

The man desiring a Pepsi is a classic example of expectations (as well as self-statements and evaluation).Expectations becomes problems when a want grows into a MUST. THE POISON WORD IS

"MUST". WHEN EVER YOU MUTTER THAT WORD IN YOUR MIND, YOU HAVE JUST MADE THE SITUATION A LIFE OR DEATH MATTER AND BECAUSE YOU HAVE, YOU WILL GO AFTER WHAT EVER IS BEFORE YOU. *TO SAY "MUST" IS TO HAVE YOUR EXPECTATIONS SET IN AN UNREAL WORLD AND CAUSE YOUR ADDICTIVE MINDSET TO CONTINUE.*

I Corinthians 13:4-7 Read this passage carefully. This is a description of perfect love, God's kind of love. He is patient, kind, and so on. He, being perfect, decided to die for us so that we don't have to be perfect anymore to relate to Him. You see, that wasn't His problem. That was our problem Adam and Eve were ashamed when they saw their own sin, and hid from God. He doesn't hide from us when we are angry; we hide from Him. We've always done that when we feel we don't measure up.

Here are the attributes of perfect love:

Patient, kind, doesn't envy, doesn't boast, isn't proud, isn't rude, isn't selfish, not easily angered, keeps no record of wrongs, doesn't delight in evil, but rejoices with the truth, protects, trusts, hopes, perseveres.

THAT IS HOW GOD RELATES TO YOU!! Let that soak in. You may have intellectually believed that, but if you are a typical addictive personality, the child within you doesn't respond as if it were true. ALL of the attributes of perfect love have to do with living with IMPERFECT PEOPLE. If people were supposed to be perfect, WHY WOULD I HAVE TO BE PATIENT, KIND, NOT BRING UP PAST WRONGS …?

HERE IS A PARADOX: FOR YOU TO BE ABLE TO DEVELOP GOD'S LOVE IN YOUR LIFE, YOU MUST LOWER YOUR EXPECTATIONS OF YOURSELF AND OTHERS. How much? Probably about 20-30%, if you are the typical addictive personality.

Look back at your Life History record. How many of the hurts or wounds you received have to do with SOMEONE NOT EXTENDING GRACE TO YOU?

IF YOUR EXPECTATIONS ARE TOO HIGH, YOU CANNOT EXTEND GRACE TO OTHERS AND YOURSELF, AND YOU CANNOT LOVE. There lies the source of much of your problem When you were hurt and made conclusions and vows, you decided:

1. Life should be a 10 if I can just get my act together and others would cooperate with me.

2. I will never be hurt again. I cannot extend grace to others and be vulnerable, because people will take advantage of me.

These mindsets will cause you to become rigid and defensive. Many things become threats that really are not. Then what is the answer?

The Great Prescription (Commandment) Matthew 22:37-40 and Romans 12:1-2

Most people misquote this passage. They leave out, "This is the first and greatest commandment." The word "command" is "entole" in the Bible. It means "*an authoritative prescription.*" Isn't that great?! It isn't do or else" thing at all. It's the medicine to make us well.

Now, if loving God with ALL my heart, soul and mind is where I'm supposed to start. I need to understand why.

Look at Romans 12:1 again. Paul says "…in view of God's mercy…offer your bodies as living sacrifices…"

THE ANSWER IS TO *ACCEPT* GOD'S GRACE TOTALLY! THEN AND ONLY THEN CAN YOU EXTEND GRACE TO OTHERS AND THEN YOURSELF--**not the other way around**! You cannot love someone with ALL of your heart, soul and mind if you look at them as someone who is hard on you. Secular thought will tell you that you have to love yourself before you can love others. That is a lie. What if you look like a frog" By secular standards you would have to get a nose job and have the warts removed; or, pump some iron and run until your little flippers fell off--but you would "look" better! How ridiculous! No amount of mental gymnastics or physical training is going to change the fact that you look like a frog and are a frog on the inside.

But, if I love God because I accept His grace; and if I remove the hard places from my heart, *I will grow the fruit of the Holy Spirit!* It doesn't matter if I look like a frog if I have love, joy, peace, patience, kindness, goodness, faithfulness, gentleness, and self-control. I can love! Further, I can love others AS I love myself. Equally. Neither more nor less than, but equally. I can lower my expectations of myself. People are going to love me back.

Expectations that are too high make us *perfectionists*. Perfectionism is not necessarily having everything in its place at home.

How many of the following statements can you identify with on a scale of 1-10? (1=not at all; 10=very much so.) REMEMBER, BE HONEST.

____ I'm often frustrated with people's performance.
____ If a job's worth doing, it's worth doing right
____ If you can't do your best, don't do it.
____ People ought to do right.
____ Things ought to go right.
____ There wouldn't be any hassles in life if people would cooperate with me.
____ There wouldn't be any hassles in my life if I could just "get it together."
____ The grammar of these questions irritates me.
____ I wish every day could be a 10.
____ I remember vacations that were ruined, or nearly ruined, because something went wrong.
____ I find myself going over things I should have done better.
____ I can't leave things alone until they are just the way I want them.
____ I believe that someday everything will go smoothly.
____ Life is really hard. Sometimes I don't know if I can make it.
____ I find myself wondering at times if I'm really doing enough for God.

____ ADD UP YOUR SCORE

50 You are a borderline perfectionist.
75 You are a perfectionist.
100 You are probably impossible to live with.
150 You are from another planet babe-come down to earth.

LOWER YOUR EXPECTATIONS OF PEOPLE AND YOURSELF!

PERFECT LOVE ACCEPTS IMPERFECT PEOPLE RIGHT WHERE THEY ARE, NOT WHERE IT WISHES THEY WERE.

It helps to accept the fact that *most people are neurotic* to some degree. That may shock you, but it is true. If you expect most people to be "perfect" and most days to be a dream, you are in for a lot of frustration.

KEYS TO LOWERING YOUR EXPECTATIONS

1. Develop a sense of humor.

Being able to laugh at yourself is a medicine. Don't take yourself so seriously. Don't take others so seriously, remember, most of them are neurotic. What they do can be very funny at times--even when they are angry with you!

2. Learn to relax.

Plan time for recreation. If you don't plan for it, then more "serious" things will press in and you will be taking life too seriously again. If someone asks you to do something that would impose on your recreation time, say you have an appointment. You do. I've never had anyone question me when I said I had an appointment.

When you recreate, don't have it planned out to the last detail. Allow for things to go wrong and also allow for spontaneity.

Get rid of all hobbies that demand perfectionism--like needlepoint, realistic art and possibly golf. These types of hobbies are OK if you can back off, but will only reinforce your perfectionism if you continue to insist you should be a scratch golfer when your handicap is 22.

3. Educate yourself about human nature and development.

If you feel you have the *right* to expect more from someone, and they can't deliver, you are going to be angry needlessly. If you are expecting something from your 4-year old that he is not able to do yet, you are going to assume he is rebelling against you.

4. Educate yourself about those around you.

You may assume you "know" them. Find out what they are good at and what they are weak in. DON'T EXPECT ANYTHING FROM THEIR WEAKNESSES. If you do, you will try to control them and blame them for your anger. If they are usually late, don't depend on them to pick you up for important appointments. You will be much happier if you depend on strengths instead of weaknesses.

PROJECT:

1. Appoint a time to sit down with your mate or best friend to talk about *his or her* strengths and weaknesses. Resolve to lower your expectations in the weak area.

2. In the space below, list the expectations that you now understand were too high on yourself and others. Share these with those people around you and make yourself accountable to them. Give them the permission to remind you if you raise your expectations again.

STEP 5. CHANGING THE ADDICTIVE LIFESTYLE

We have now come to the last step in your healing. YOU NOW HAVE THE ABILITY TO CHANGE YOUR ADDICTIVE LIFESTYLE—BEFORE YOU DIDN'T. Remember, men and women are changed first by a spiritual transformation, followed by a renewing of the mind, and last of all, by reinforcing their new perspective by ACTING ON IT. Without a period of conscientious application of the new truths in your life, you will go back to your old patterns. Why? Because much of your old life was a habit. You became comfortable acting that way. If it takes 21 repetitions to form a habit, it will take some time of walking in your new perspective to feel completely natural in it. *At first, it will feel awkward.* It is right here that many well-meaning people miss the way. They fail to realize that the child within them has run their lives by **emotion.** They have formed the habit of following their emotions. The child within has to be retrained. He has to be bridled and not allowed to walk in ways that are disruptive to the "family". These people do things because they feel like it, or wait to do things they know they should until they feel like it. Knowledge of truth alone doesn't change people. Some of the most intelligent people in the world do illogical things. I remember being on the staff of a hospital and hearing about the tumor board. This is a group of specialists from every department of the hospital who review cancer cases before surgery to determine if the surgery is necessary. One morning a case to remove a man's left lung was being reviewed. It was hopelessly cancerous from years of cigarette smoking. EVERY SURGEON IN THAT ROOM WAS SMOKING!! They each had an addiction.

Walking in wholeness is a MOTOR SKILL. A motor skill is something you do naturally without really thinking about it. You don't learn to use a typewriter by reading about it or talking about it. No, first you read about it and then begin to apply what you know by practice. Only after a period of trial and error can you say, "I know how to type." It is only after much more practice that you feel natural at the keyboard. It is something like that for you. New patterns will stick only if you practice. This is true because of a basic, Biblical truth:

EMOTIONS FOLLOW ACTION

That is why God's commands are a prescription to you for healing. If you don't take the medicine, you can't expect to get well. Before going on, let's look at some scriptures that talk about this truth:

John 15:10-12   What do you see as the prerequisite for remaining in God's love in these verses?

Is the word "love" in these verses a noun or a verb?

What is the promise if you do this?

Does the promise come before or after your acting?

Matt. 7:24-28   What do you see as the prerequisite for withstanding stress in your life in these verses?

What are the consequences of not putting these words into action?

Does the promise come before or after your acting?

James 1:22-25   What do you see as the connection between hearing the healing words of God and being able to remember them?

What is the promise?

James 2:14-26   What do you think James is saying here about the connection between having spiritual life and death?

Enough said. Let's start discussing specific things you must do to retrain the child within. Please understand that each of the following points, are projects that are going to be an ongoing reality in your life. *You must be aggressive in applying them!* You must be especially vigilant in the first three months after you start this. It will take you that long to form new habits. New habits are formed by reinforcing them with action, *constantly.*

1. FACE YOUR FEARS

As you have learned, anger most often springs out of fear. We feel insecure or anxious, so we lash out to defend ourselves. Some of us internalize our anger and grow more and more angry at ourselves for not taking control of our lives. This leads to low self-esteem. IT IS THE SELF-BLAME AND CONDEMNATION YOU HEAP ON YOURSELF FOR NOT DOING ANYTHING ABOUT YOUR FEARS THAT CAUSE YOUR POOR SELF IMAGE. YOU FEEL POWERLESS. Therefore, building your self-confidence will help you resist emotional outburst.

PROJECT:

On a piece of paper, list all your fears. Don't worry about the order at this stage, but do include your "people" fears. It doesn't matter how silly you might think they are, list as many of your fears as you can. Now, on the next page is a form, place your fears in ascending order, i.e., from your smallest fear to your biggest.

If it becomes confusing to you which ones are bigger than others, ask yourself this question: "What would it take to make me do......."? For me, it would almost take a gun to my head to make me climb out on a high ledge without a harness around me secured to a very sturdy anchor.

Next, DO SOMETHING ABOUT EACH ONE. WORK DOWN THE LADDER. Keep doing each one until you lose your fear. You will be amazed what this does for your self-confidence!! The reason for this is that you will start to realize that you can control your life. But, you are not likely to start with your medium or big fears—that would be too much. Yet, that is exactly why you haven't started this before. By starting with the smallest fears, you can work up to the big ones.

If you come to one that you can't face alone, have a friend or pastor go with you. If you have a fear of driving a car, have a friend sit with you while you back up and drive forward in your driveway. Next go to an empty parking lot.

FEAR	WHAT I'M GOING TO DO

2. BREAKING OFF ADDICTIVE RELATIONSHIPS:

There is probably no greater influence in your life than acquaintances of yours who use drugs or drink. What you must keep in mind is that they have an elaborate denial system just like you used to have. *They may say they are happy for you when you tell them you are part of Freedom Now and have started your path of healing. But, if they are addicted, they will try to influence you to use again because your quitting makes them feel uneasy.* YOU WILL FIND THAT WHEN YOU QUIT, THESE PEOPLE ARE NOT YOUR FRIENDS ANYMORE. IN CONCLUSSION, WHAT WAS THE BASIS OF YOUR FRIENDSHIP BEFORE USING? **THE DRUG.**

The common bond of users is the drug. If you continue to be with them, you will use again. In our group, I have lost track of the number of people who have fallen again because they believed they were the exception to this rule. TO PERMANENTLY CHANGE, YOU MUST CHANGE YOUR LIFESTYLE.

Project: Look at the following questionnaire and check those items that still apply to you.

    ___My friends are mainly users.
    ___I feel awkward about forming new friendships who are not users.
    ___I still have drug paraphernalia (bongs, etc.) in my car or house.
    ___I still dress and wear my hair in a way that identifies with the drug culture.
    ___I still have the phone numbers of my dealers.
    ___When I talk about my drug use, I laugh or joke about it.

How bad do you really want to change? These are all things that must go if you are really serious.

3. CHANGING THE WAY YOU EAT:

If you have been using chemicals to replace the fruit of the Holy Spirit, your body is a biochemical mess! God wants you to be healed in your body as well as your spirit and emotions. However, our bodies won't heal if we continue to abuse them.

The biochemistry of the addict or alcoholic has been radically altered and has been so dependent on the presence of the chemical, that normal metabolism has been altered or has shut down. There has been:[14]

1. Malnutrition – Calorie needs have not been met. The appetite center of your brain has been anesthetized so that you don't feel hungry even when your body needs food.

2. Organ damage – Your liver, brain tissue and other organs have been damaged to some extent or other.

3. Systemic toxicity – *Every drug, whether it is intended for medical treatment or not, has an LD 50 dosage.* This is the dose that will **kill** 50% of the rats given that dose. If it will kill a rat, think of what it did to your system. In fact when you were using, the toxicity level in your system was so high, *you could not think straight.* It wasn't that you didn't want to, you couldn't! That is why we told you not to be afraid or embarrassed about going into the hospital to be de-toxified.

4. Neurochemical imbalances – Because of the neurotransmitter interference and toxicity, your system was not able to function properly. Thinking processes, reflexes and senses were all affected.

5. Immunological imbalances – Your ability to fight off disease is altered by drugs and alcohol.

6. Endocrine malfunctions – Because of neurotransmitter interference and toxicity, your body has been hampered in its ability to make the vital hormones necessary. In advanced stages, men become impotent and women cease their menstrual cycle.

God has made your body in a wonderful way. There are two truths to remember regarding your chemistry:

1. **Balance: Your body will** *always* **react to keep itself in balance. When outside chemicals are taken in that interfere or mimic its natural biochemical, it will quit making its own or try to compensate in some way. However, it can't compensate to maintain health.** *It can only compensate to survive!* **So, when nicotine, caffeine, sugar or any other chemical is introduced that interferes or mimics your body's natural chemicals, your chemistry is thrown out of balance.** There will be an initial rush with these outside chemicals, but the downside will be terrible because the natural chemicals have been shut down.[15]

2. **Design: God has designed your body so that** *for every high that a drug can produce, there is a natural biological equivalent, already present in your body that will make you feel better, and last longer WITH NO UNPLEASANT SIDE EFFECTS.*[16] Therefore, learning to fine tune your body without any outside influence can be a liberating quest. Think of it--you don't have to rely on any outside influence!

The "feel good" chemicals that your body makes are endorphins, enkephalins and serotonin. All these are hampered by poor nutrition.

Nutrition and mood swings: We are attempting to get you to see that just as your addiction to chemicals altered your mood, so can food. Food is the number one drug of choice in America. We don't want you to trade one addiction for another. *But we definitely want you to understand that old eating habits can throw you back into your addiction if you don't change them.*

YOUR BLOOD GLUCOSE LEVEL is one of *the* determining factors in your mood swings. If you were an alcoholic, your brain learned to use alcohol instead of glucose for fuel. This eventually impaired or even destroyed your carbohydrate metabolism. The addict, typically has a diet high in junk food, caffeine and nicotine to give him that feeling of "energy".[17] He's like a police car with all the sirens running but the motor has run out of gas and oil.[18]

As a result of this short lived and artificial energy food source, there is a drastic swing in blood glucose levels with intermittent highs and crashes. The neurotransmitter levels are also affected, 60-90% of people in this predicament will suffer symptoms of depression. Many have been misdiagnosed as bipolar.

Disturbed glucose levels have been linked to low levels of **serotonin** (mood-regulating neurochemical). *Low* serotonin levels have been linked to depressive syndromes and may account for the high suicide rates among addicts.[19]

So what does this have to do with you? Plenty. All chemical dependent groups will tell you to avoid four things in restructuring your lifestyle:

1. **H**unger

2. **A**nger

3. **L**oneliness

4. **T**iredness

Taking care of your body with proper rest and nutrition is more important than you might think. When you are hungry, you're irritable. When you are irritable, you're susceptible.

There was a study done by a Dr. R. Guenther in 1982 that dealt with alcoholics. The test group received vitamin supplements and nutritional guidance. The control group did not. Both groups received the usual inpatient and outpatient care. After six months, 60% of the test group was still clean and sober while only 20% of the control group was. The difference was that the test group had brought their metabolism into balance. The control group did not.[20]

Let's start looking at some simple, practical things you can do to change your metabolism.

CARDINAL RULES TO NUTRITIONAL FREEDOM:

1. **3-0-1 :** This stands for 3 meals a day; 0 in between meals; one day at a time.

> Your body has a preset biorhythm for three meals a day. When you eat in between meals, you upset this rhythm, your appetite center in your brain becomes confused and you start to lose your ability to distinguish between being "body hungry" (your body is demanding food) and "mouth hungry" (an addiction to food symptom). Your blood glucose levels fluctuate because between meal snacks are typically junk food, high in calories and low in food value. Even if they are nutritious, your body doesn't need them and something has to be done with the calories so they are stored for later use. To do this, your carbohydrate and protein metabolism is called into service when they are already doing what they were intended to do. As a consequence, you put an unnecessary load on your metabolism, "confuse it" and store fat. (Note: If you are a diabetic, or have other blood glucose disorders, your metabolism will not allow you to do this—consult your physician.)

> Dr. W. Swarner of the Eating Disorder clinic of Portland Adventist Medical Center says that it is very difficult to overeat if you only eat three meals a day. You can eat all you want, but only at meals. I have tried this and found it to be true. I feel stuffed and am just starting to become "body" hungry before the next meal. I also lost 20 pounds!

2. **Cut out artificial chemicals,** such as caffeine, nicotine and sucrose (white sugar). As we have seen, these outside chemicals replace some of our natural neurochemicals and cause us to "crash" after their withdrawal. If we continue to use them, we still are not free from outside control and haven't really allowed this marvelous body of ours to function as it was intended. If you have a "incurable sweet tooth", have your dessert with meals—not in between meals.

3. **Start feeding your body what it needs:** Recent research has confirmed a lot of suspicions and blown a lot of myths right out the window!

> First of all, the good old American diet we were told was good for us after World War II, isn't. Diets high in meat and dairy products produce heart disease and cancer. The healthiest diets in the world are those found in southern Italy and in parts of China.

> The diet of southern Italy is high in pasta and bread and fruits and vegetables. The diet in China is high in vegetables.

> Both diets are low in meat and dairy products. Our bodies don't require large amounts of meat for the needed protein. **The culprit is foods with high amounts** *fat*! Counting calories all the time can cause you to be consumed by the subject of food. After a while, you will find yourself being addicted to food because you have to think about it all the time or you will put on those unsightly pounds.[21]

> It is much healthier to eat for health—not looks. Just watch your fat intake.

4. START EXERCISING:

Your metabolism doesn't function properly unless it's challenged. One thing you may have noticed throughout the last pages is THAT YOUR BODY IS SMARTER THAN YOU ARE. It knows what it needs if you will listen to it. It will always do what is necessary to survive on its own. So, when you are sedentary it interprets the lack of demand on itself as preparation for famine and stores up fat at a faster rate than it would if you were doing some mild exercise.

But, here is the good news! Recent research shows us that you don't have to kill yourself to exercise. Aren't you glad for that? In fact, when you vow to yourself that you are going to jog, and go out that first day and get winded and almost throw up, do you know what your body does? It interprets that episode as being under *unnatural* stress and starts storing up fat because it thinks you are in a famine! That's why people who go out and start exercising too strenuously, find they put on weight faster after they stop.

WHAT'S THE ANSWER? Moderate, aerobic exercise. **This varies from person to person. It equals the exercise you can do and still talk in short bursts.** At this rate of exercise, you will burn fat. Anything beyond being able to talk in short burst while exercising pushes you in to anaerobic (without oxygen) exercise which winds you (oxygen debt) and your system starts burning blood glucose instead of fat. As soon as the blood glucose is burned up and the lactic acid builds up in your muscles, you crash and "hit the wall". This causes the pain you feel during strenuous exercise that only the masochists like. That pain isn't necessary to fitness! You can be aerobically fit with exercise in moderate amounts. Walking, cycling, swimming are marvelous. Just maintain the "talking in short bursts" rule for at least 30 minutes every other day.

If you want to lose fat faster, start building up your muscles with weight training. Muscles burn fat. The larger the muscles, the more fat they burn. This is why men can lose fat faster than women—they have more muscle mass. If you are a woman, *accept that your body is set to carry around 23% body fat because of your hormones.* For you to be at 12% body fat, you would have to exercise every day, most of the day. The models you see in magazines and on TV, are *unnatural.* Many of them are anorexic and or bulimic. If you try to copy them, you will end up in a food addiction.[22]

5. BUILD COPING SKILLS:

Remember, we live in an imperfect world. People will do and say things that will upset you. You can't change them because you are not God, and you can't live without them. Therefore, you have to learn to live with them.

A. Learn to handle negative input.

The Genius Principle. A genius is smart enough to know that morons or "Hitlers" may have something of value to say; they may be totally off base in most areas, but they may have a small handle on truth in others. Geniuses are gleaners of information that may benefit THEM. They separate truth from the person. They are champions of the truth.

This allows them to do a very interesting thing. It keeps them from being diverted from their purpose, their potential. They are not swayed by whether they like or dislike a person. They are able to focus their potential in one direction, gathering information as they go. They never assume that they "have arrived." They are constantly looking for ways to improve.

But, here is the surprising truth! Literally tens of thousands of people have IQ's in the genius class. *It is only the ones that put what we are saying here into practice that we recognize as "genius".* In other words, they reach their potential.

When someone confronts them with criticism, they separate the *person* from what is said, and go through two steps in their minds:

    a. *Is it true?*

If it is true, they accept it. It will help them be better people.

Do you think a genius is a humble person? Why?

To reach your potential--everything God created you to be--you must repent when people point out your faults. Watch out for defensiveness!

    b. *Is it false?*

If it is false, they reject it. It is not information what will help them.

Practice telling people you are sorry they feel badly about you, but you don't see it their way. Thank them for their concern and refuse to defend yourself.

A genius is able to process false information by evaluation. If he has searched his heart and the accusations come up false, *then the accuser has the problem.*

        He either:
                Has wrong information.
                Is warped (neurotic).
                Has been sent by the devil.

AS SOON AS YOU DEFEND YOURSELF AGAINST FALSE ACCUSATIONS IN ANGER, YOU HAVE TAKEN THAT PERSON'S *PROBLEM ON YOURSELF!*

People have the right to be wrong. People have the right to be neurotic. Let them have their problem. Don't try to take it away from them to make you feel better.

B. Be assertive--not hostile.

Assertiveness is a positive way to channel anger into productive avenues. It's doing something about your anger. Assertiveness *is not* hostility. It is remaining calm, positive but firm. It does not judge or condemn the other person, but simply states its desires in the matter. It does not escalate its desires to demands if the matter cannot be resolved.

Luke 17:1-4 What is Jesus saying to do here?

Verse 5---Why do you think the disciples reacted this way?

Matt. 18:15 & Eph. 4 25-27 What is God's solution to not letting the sun go down on your anger?

C. Don't allow other people to control you.

Sometimes, those who come to you with false information won't give up. They are like junkyard dogs--they are protecting something and chewing up people. Every time you come near them, they try to chew on you. They are insecure, fearful people. They will do practically anything to get their way.

    a. Resist revenge: Luke 6:37,38.

      Please read this carefully. Realize *that they will be judged; they will be condemned.* You do not want to take their sin upon yourself by playing God. Payday always comes.
      "Vengeance is mine, I will repay, says the Lord." (Rom. 12:19 ESV)

    b. Enforce logical consequences.

      Junk yard dogs will choke themselves if you give them enough chain. Unless they suffer for their mistakes, they will keep making them. When you turn on a junkyard dog, he feels JUSTIFIED in his viciousness. Walk away. Let him hit the end of his chain. TRUTH WILL PREVAIL.

    Example:

    You have been constantly frustrated with an individual who is angry. He butts in and won't let you finish sentences. You are trying to tell him something important that will affect him directly in the next day or so, but he won't listen. What should you do?

    c. Slow down!

      Counting to 10 really works. From now on, try not to react instantaneously. Be slow to anger. When you feel impulsive, **stop** and put into practice everything you have learned.

      Take timeouts. If you try to slow down, but the other person won't back off, tell him you need a time out and walk away. Don't spend the time away as an escape; spend it deciding how you are going to attempt to resolve the conflict by the things you have learned. But remember, you can't resolve things with everyone.

6. BUILD COMFORT AND PREDICTABILITY INTO YOUR LIFE:

You have learned that the root of your addiction had to do with unmet needs and trauma from your past. Even if this wasn't a strong factor in your addiction, the truth is that now you have lost structure in your life and you were anesthetizing your pain by running from it. Drugs were the escape.

Now, you must give yourself permission to build comfort into your life WITH HEALTHY ALTERNATIVES.

LIST SOME THINGS IN THIS SPACE THAT YOU ALWAYS WANTED TO DO, BUT HAVEN'T:
Things like traveling, taking a college course etc..

Next, make plans now for *starting* to move towards one of those "want to" goals. Don't worry about whether it seems feasible! What is the first step?

Project: Go back in this manual to the exercise where you got in touch with your issues. In the chart below, name the unmet need and then plan to do something about meeting that need. Tell someone what you have decided.

Issue	Unmet Need	How I plan to meet that need	When

STRUCTURE YOUR TIME:

One of the symptoms of growing up in an alcoholic and/or dysfunctional family is being impulsive. *It is a prolonged temper tantrum.* Everything you were kept from doing you do, and everything you were made to do, you don't—even if it is good for you. Whenever you feel constrained, confined or restricted, you throw off the restrictions just to show everyone you are in control. The problem is that after a while, these behaviors become addictive and you end up just like your alcoholic parent.

Therefore, don't continue to let your emotions rule you with your free time. Addicts will say, "When I get a day off, I'm going to do only what I want to do!" This usually translates, "I'm going to do nothing!" However, when the time comes, they are frustrated because doing "nothing" isn't fulfilling and they end up lonely, anxious and are tempted to use again. They are often throwing a temper tantrum they are not even aware of. When this happens, loneliness and anger build up and they have fallen into the relapse trap. So structure your free time. Plan to have fun. You are in control.

1. Schedule at least one enjoyable event per evening or other free time.

2. Plan each day *in advance.*

7. GET INVOLVED WITH HELPING OTHERS:

Putting on the new man has to do with imitating Christ. He shows us how we are wired to live. It is as we imitate Him that we find true fulfillment. It isn't easy but it is fulfilling.

Hans Selye, the father of modern stress physiology, concluded after all of his research on the subject that people were the most fulfilled, the most at ease, when they were involved in what he coined **benevolent philanthropy.** What is that? Giving to others with the motive of love.

The addictive personality is self-absorbed, introspective—very much into itself. Healing never ultimately comes that way. That is why psychoanalysis can go on for years without much improvement. Hans Selye discovered what our Lord recorded in the Bible thousands of years ago:

> **John 15:9-13** As the Father has loved me, so have I loved you. Abide in my love. If you keep my commandments, you will abide in my love, just as I have kept my Father's commandments and abide in his love. These things I have spoken to you, **that my joy may be in you, and that your joy may be full.** "This is my commandment, that you love one another as I have loved you. Greater love has no one than this, that someone lay down his life for his friends.

8. CONTINUE GROWING SPIRITUALLY:

Resist the tendency to hold on to Jesus as your life preserver. He delivered you but He wants to be much more than your life preserver. Growing the fruit of the Holy Spirit is a process. It grows as you continue to walk in obedience to the Holy Spirit and scripture. The complete cure is to be so full of the Holy Spirit that you wouldn't ever want to go back to drugs. Once you have experienced the fullness of God in your life, you'll never need anything else.

This class was not intended to give you that growth. Move on in the Church and get involved with other Christians besides those who have been healed of addictions. Your church should have all sorts of opportunities.

RELAPSE PREVENTION

Our experience is that many people are set free from their cravings immediately after their confession and house cleaning for the healing of the addictive root.

Our experience also tells us that some do not apply themselves to changing their addictive mindset and eventually start experiencing old patterns again. For those individuals, going through the housecleaning again and then healing the addictive mindset is necessary.

For some, their experience is one of cycling through this healing process several times before they are totally free.

Whatever your experience happens to be, we want you *not* to be ignorant about relapse and recognizing its onset. To not mention this to you would be foolish. The question is how do you recognize it, and more importantly, how do you prevent it?

MYTHS ABOUT RELAPSE:

1. Relapse is a sign of failure.
> No it isn't. You made a mistake. Try again

2. Relapse is sign of poor motivation.
> No it isn't. It sometimes is part of addiction showing itself in the healing process.

3. Relapse starts as soon as you pick up that drug or drink.
> No it doesn't. It starts a long time before that.

4. Relapse is unpredictable and unavoidable.
> No it isn't. There are numerous red flags ahead of time.

5. Relapse only involves the drug of choice.
> No it doesn't. Addictions usually have partners. Sexual addictions and other mood changers can trigger the path to relapse.

6. Relapse cancels out all the progress you've made.
> No it doesn't. It only points out how vulnerable you are.

7. If relapse doesn't cancel out my progress, then it is OK to have one.
> No it isn't. You will spiral into helplessness again.

BATTLE PLAN:

You need to have a battle plan just in case. If you get to the point where you are on the front porch of your dealer or driving up to your old tavern, it's too late. If you find yourself in a situation and you are struggling *not* to use, follow these tried and true steps:

1. Leave!
> Simple, but a must. Don't kid yourself into thinking you can handle it.

2. Get ahold of your Freedom Now support system. Have them pray with you.

3. Detach.
> Isolate your thoughts and person from that environment. It may mean you will have to take your phone off the hook/shut it off or not answer your door.

4. Time Management.

   Take control of your time so that you don't have free time to be alone and vulnerable.

5. Think about the *negative* consequences if you used again. List them.

6. Record the steps of your near fall so that you are aware next time.

7. Relax.

   Take a hot bath. Go jogging. Read the promises of God again. Watch a movie. Do whatever you need to do to relax, *except using mood altering chemicals.*

8. See yourself winning!

   With what you know now, and with God's help, you most definitely are going to win.

RECOGNIZING THE RELAPSE CHAIN:

SEQUENTIAL STEPS IN RELAPSE	DIAGNOSIS/COUNTERMEASURES
1. The buildup of stress.	Haven't done a thorough house cleaning or changed the addictive mindset. Not using the coping skills
2. Emotional overreaction.	The emotional outburst is a reaction to a perceived life or death situation. It isn't. Same reasons as step 1. Should get hold of support immediately.
3. Denial sets in. Person starts to stuff their feelings and shut down.	You are trying to be omnipotent. You feel if you try not to think about it, it will go away. You need to talk out your thoughts and your feelings with someone and have them pray. James 5:16
4. Failure to get support.	Omnipotence. Guilt and shame.
5. Little lies start to creep in.	You are starting to build up a defense mechanism again to protect what they are contemplating doing. After a while, they start believing their own lies and deceive themselves. This adds to the denial. Hardness of heart has started to set in again.
6. Increased isolation.	Omnipotence. It still isn't too late to reach out.
7. Problems grow worse because you will not seek help.	Omnipotence. Rage at self and others. Problems not only seem more serious, they often are.
8. Hopelessness	You are starting to panic because you cannot get a handle on your emotions. Reach out. Humble yourself.
9. Self-sabotage. You deliberately get into high risk situations.	Omnipotence. You believe that because you can't get a handle on this yourself, you might as well give in.
10. Use	
11. Defeatist reaction.[23]	Believe that because you relapsed, you were destined to be an addict and always will be. Relapse is not the end. Healing begins again. You need to go through the healing cycle again.

CRAVINGS OR RELAPSE *DO NOT* MEAN THIS HEALING PROCESS ISN'T WORKING. *REMEMBER, THERE IS NO QUICK FIX*! RELAPSES ARE OFTEN PART OF THE ADDICTIVE HEALING PROCESS. REACH OUT, LET OTHERS HELP YOU UP, LEAN ON GOD AND LEARN FROM THE EXPERIENCE.

This concludes this manual. We sincerely pray that your later years will be greater than your former years and that you are in the process of finding your niche in God's kingdom. God bless you! We would love to hear from you by letter. Drop us a line and let us know how you are doing.

People who have hurt me:

People I have hurt:

Sins, bondages & problems I am struggling with now:

Age	Feeling	Incident

1. Washton, Arnold, Ph.D., & Donna Boundy, *Will Power is Not Enough*, New York, Harper and Row, 1989, pg. 45.

2. Washton, pg. 53.

3. Washton, pp. 19-25.

4. Washton, pp. 33-43.

5. Beasley, Joseph, M.D., How To Defeat Alcoholism, Random House, 1989. Pg. 31.

6. Washton, pg. 45.

7. Beasley pg. 30.

8. Washton, pp. 50-67.

9. Johnson, Theo, *New Images*, East Hill Church, 1990. Pp. 5-6.

10. Sandford, John and Paula, *The Transformation Of the Inner Man*, Bridge Publishing Inc., 1982, pp. 237-238.

11. Adapted from audio tape by John Sandford, *The Wounded Spirit*, 1984.

12. Sandford, audio tape, *The Wounded Spirit*, 1984.

13. Washton, pg. 60.

14. Beasley, pp. 19-21.

15. Beasley, pp. 30-32.

16. Beasley, pg. 30.

17. Beasley, pp. 52-53.

18. Swarner, Warner, M.D., May 24, 1991, conference at Warner Pacific College, Portland, Oregon.

19. Beasley, pg. 52.

20. Beasley, pg. 21.

21. Adapted from the video, "Eat Smart", Judy Woodruff host, MacNeil-Leherer Productions, Boston, 1991.

22. Bailey, Covert & Lea Bishop, *The Fit Or Fat Woman*, Houghton & Mifflin Co., 1989. Pp.42-44.

23. Washton, pp. 197-203.

Made in the USA
Middletown, DE
27 April 2022

64853166R00051